Thread Painting
MADE EASY

TERRY
WHITE

American Quilter's Society
P. O. Box 3290 • Paducah, KY 42002-3290
www.AmericanQuilter.com

Located in Paducah, Kentucky, the American Quilter's Society (AQS) is dedicated to promoting the accomplishments of today's quilters. Through its publications and events, AQS strives to honor today's quiltmakers and their work and to inspire future creativity and innovation in quiltmaking.

Text © 2008, Author, Terry White
Artwork © 2008, American Quilter's Society

EXECUTIVE EDITOR: NICOLE C. CHAMBERS
SENIOR EDITOR: LINDA BAXTER LASCO
GRAPHIC DESIGN: ELAINE WILSON
COVER DESIGN: MARY BETH HEAD
PHOTOGRAPHY: CHARLES R. LYNCH
HOW-TO PHOTOGRAPHY: TERRY WHITE

American Quilter's Society
P. O. Box 3290 • Paducah, KY 42002-3290
www.AmericanQuilter.com

Additional copies of this book may be ordered from the American Quilter's Society, PO Box 3290, Paducah, KY 42002-3290, or online at www.AmericanQuilter.com.

LIBRARY OF CONGRESS CATALOGING-IN-PUBLICATION DATA

White, Terry.
  Thread painting made easy / by Terry White.
     p. cm.
  ISBN 978-1-57432-950-6
  1. Embroidery, Machine--Patterns. I. Title.

TT772.W53 2008
746.44'041--dc22

2008018016

Proudly printed and bound in the United States of America

Dedication

This book is dedicated to the people who supported me. I got pretty heavy at times, which is why I needed all of them. They believed in me (when I didn't) and they knew just the right things to say and do at just the right times. Even though they tease me, I know they love me (pretty sure). I consider myself blessed, honored, and very lucky to have them in my life.

To:

My husband, Scot

My sister, Mary Ann

My brother, Wally

My daughter, Robby

My mother-in-law, Jean

My father-in-law, Bob

I am very grateful.

I love you.

Acknowledgments

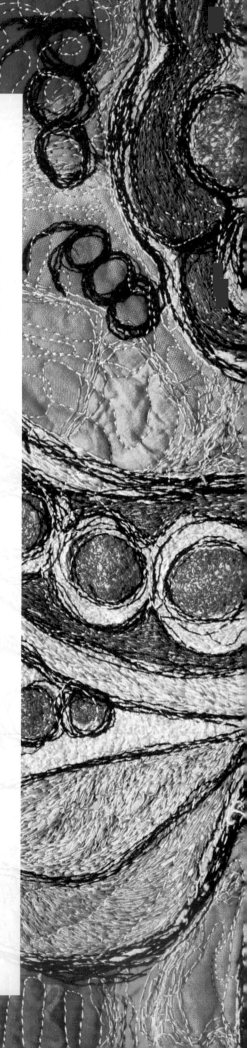

A big "Thank you!" goes to all my students. The questions that people ask in the classroom help me to define my reasons for doing things or using specific materials. I may find that a certain needle or thread works best, but I need to know the reason why in order to communicate it to others. Classroom discoveries are great catalysts for new ideas.

Thank you Meredith Schroeder, Bonnie Browning, and Nicole Chambers. I want you to know that you helped to make one of my biggest dreams come true. I've wanted to write a book on needlework since I was seventeen (which was a very long time ago).

Thank you Joe Snyder of Singer Sewing Machine Company for providing me with the Singer XL-6000. It's a great machine for my techniques.

Thank you Andrew Ngai and Liz Kettle of Wonderfil Threads for the beautiful threads and the opportunity to work with you great people.

Thank you Jane Garrison of YLI Corporation for providing the cool threads, especially the Monet and those beautiful cotton variegates.

Thank you Heather and Bob Purcell of Superior Threads for your great support and providing King Tut variegated cotton threads. It is such a great line.

Thank you Cynthia and David John for providing the Valdani threads. I'll get those patterns to you just as soon as I finish them.

Thank you my bestest friend Sharon Schamber (and Gene, of course!) for your support, kindness, and kicking of the behind. You knew I'd write this book and get it out there even when I wasn't so sure. I knew you were the best quilter in the world before the world knew it. I must say that the basket of chocolates came in the nick of time.

Thank you to Linda Baxter Lasco who gets the gold star, to Elaine Wilson for her patience and for going the extra mile, and to Charles Lynch for his great quilt photography.

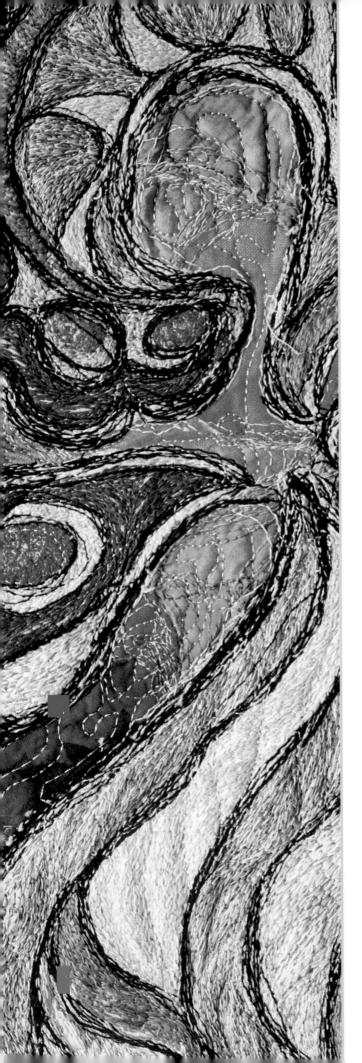

Contents

Introduction

I WANT TO TELL YOU SOMETHING.

I spent numerous years stitching embroideries by hand. I loved forming stitches with all those beautiful threads: perle cotton, linen thread, cotton floss, Persian wool, silk, gold thread, etc. The many forms of embroidery have always fascinated me. As I learned the various techniques, I studied the history of needlework and its indigenous forms around the world. My work included crewel, needlepoint, rug making, charted work, drawn threadwork, knitting, crochet, tatting, and needle lace.

Free-motion embroidery is as old as the sewing machine. I have found articles from old needlework magazines dating from the 1920s complete with pictures, patterns, and instructions for accomplishing beautiful machine embroidery. There are several embroidery books in my collection from the 1960s and '70s which include wonderful modern designs using this technique.

My first experience came from a class in the mid-eighties with Lois Smith. At the time, I didn't pursue the technique because I was doing other things. I only turned to the sewing machine in the early nineties when I could no longer work by hand.

When I thread paint, my goal is to create fiber art. I want the work to look like embroidery—because it is embroidery. Rather than mimic the work I've previously done, I'm constantly referencing my old hand work in order to create a whole new and different needle art form.

I have been a quilter for 29 years. My favorite techniques have included hand appliqué, hand embroidery, hand quilting, and machine strip piecing. I liked to make quilts with pictures on them. I have found that using thread painting, I can make pictures that I could previously only imagine.

HOOP YOUR FABRIC, THREAD YOUR MACHINE, DROP THE FEED TEETH, AND GO!

That's all you need to know to get started. When you first learn any technique, there are always a few extra bits of information that help to get the ball rolling. That's exactly what this book is about. I've spent ten years exploring this needle art form. Every time a new thread comes along, I have to try it and every time I learn something new. With every new project and every conversation with a fellow stitcher, with the time spent studying the works of artists, painters, potters, weavers, and woodcarvers, I find new inspiration. I believe that you don't really know something until you have tried it. The key to thread painting is PLAYTIME!

Thread painting is easy to learn, though it would take a lifetime to understand all the wonderful effects you can achieve. We have a lot to look forward to!

Each point of information that is in this book is a key to good work. In my classes, I have found that when someone wants to sidestep a foundation point, they always have trouble. Throughout the book, each point of information builds on the next. You won't find me saying, "Now THIS is important," or "this one is REALLY important," because it's all important to building a solid foundation. In the end, it's all about the work.

Be patient with yourself. As grown-ups we think that we should be able to pick up new things easily and instantly be successful with them. If you are a beginner, give yourself time to experiment and become familiar with the feel of the technique. Practice makes it more familiar (not perfect).

Nana's Garden
48" x 48", (detail on pages 2–3). *This quilt represents the birds, butterflies, and plants in my garden. I am Nana. The lace motif encircling the design mimics a crochet doily.* FROM THE COLLECTION OF PAUL AND SUE WHITTEAD

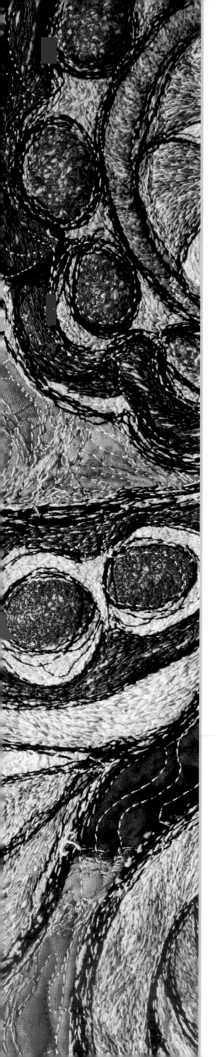

SECTION I
How to Thread Paint

A GOOD SEWING MACHINE IS A JOY FOREVER

Every sewing machine is as different as the person using it. When I started doing free-motion work, I had to buy a new machine. My Old Betsy had been faithful for ten years, but she didn't have the stitch quality I needed. Now, she's been retired to my grown daughter's house where she sews curtains and pillows. One of the best decisions I ever made was to find a sewing machine that perfectly matched my creative process.

Technology is changing all of the time, but newer does not always mean better for thread painting. Some older mechanical machines have beautiful stitch quality whereas certain computerized sewing machines don't like free-motion work. I can't tell you why, except that I know it to be true from my many classes. Personally, I love my computerized sewing machine. Its features add to the ease of my work.

If you decide to buy a new machine, my best advice is to go to the various sewing machine dealers with threads and fabrics in hand. Try out all the machines in your price range. Test the sewing techniques that you will be doing most frequently. If you feel uncertain, ask the employees for help on how to do the techniques you will be using. Buying a new sewing machine is like buying a car; you're also buying the dealer and the service department. Be sure you like them. Tell them what you want instead of buying what they want to sell you. Finding the right machine is true love!

Your machine should have good stitch quality, that is, the tension is consistently good, stitches don't skip, and threads don't (usually) break. Some machines are very good at piecing but do not work well with thread painting.

This happens when the machine has rigid tension on the top that does not allow the free flow of threads.

Drop the feed teeth or cover them up. This way, the action of the feed teeth doesn't interfere with the free-motion of the work. If the feed teeth are left up and exposed, they will brush against the bottom of your work, causing a lot of fuzz that will mess with your stitches and cause nests of knots.

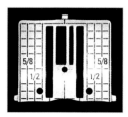

Use a single stitch needle plate. This book focuses on **straight-stitch embroidery.** In other words, the machine is always set for straight stitch. A single hole needle plate stabilizes your work, ensuring good stitch quality. The single hole needle plate has a small opening that allows the needle to pass through in the center needle position. When you have this plate on your machine, put a big note to that effect on your machine when you walk away, so that you don't come back and accidentally zig-zag something and break a needle.

Not all machines have a single hole needle plate. If your machine has good tension it is not completely necessary. If you are doing a lot of overstitching and you find you need one, you can create a single hole needle plate by piercing a small hole in a piece of plastic and taping it over the existing needle plate.

A darning foot is essential. It stabilizes the fabric on the top. It prevents the needle from pulling the fabric up into the air or pulling bobbin thread up and creating big tension headaches. An open-toe darning foot makes it very easy to see the details of the work as you stitch.

Use a thread stand for big heavy spools. This is essential when using any of the big spools of thread that don't fit in our domestic sewing machines. The weight of the spool can cause extra tension when stitching off the side. A stand aids in smooth thread delivery. Find a good metal one; the plastic ones wobble and don't help in the delivery process. Some thread stands are made to deliver more than one thread at a time. This is especially good for stitching with two threads at the same time.

Extension table. A big flat surface helps to stabilize the hoop. If you have your machine set into a table, you are very lucky. I wish I were you.

MACHINE SETUP FOR FREE-MOTION EMBROIDERY

Your machine should be clean. You should regularly clean out the bobbin case and the area around it. With thread painting, fuzz regularly collects around the bobbin case and causes trouble.

Set your machine for straight stitch.

Set your needle thread tension between 2.0 and 2.6. This should be your starting point. Test stitch to see what adjustments need to be made. Every machine is different. Your final settings could be zero or even three.

Some machines have a free-motion menu. This is a wonderful feature. Just follow the directions in your manual.

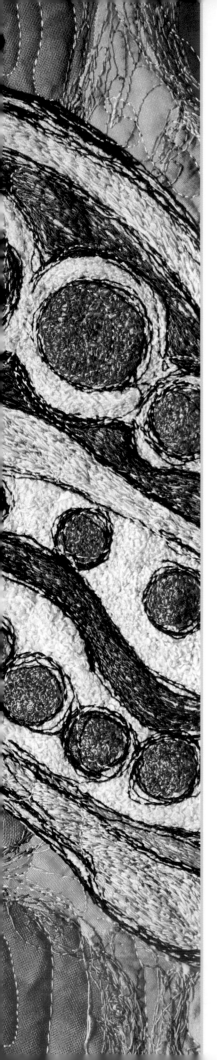

Some machines need the stitch length set to its longest setting. Even though the feed teeth are down, this adjustment makes a better tension.

Some machines have a darning setting (not darning stitch) or an adjusted setting for the darning foot. Check your manual.

Some machines have a problem with the fine bobbin thread used in machine embroidery. In this case use 50-weight sewing cotton or Maxi-Lock® thread.

AVOID TENSION HEADACHES AND THREAD BREAKS

Bad tension will cause problems in your work, not to mention your neck and your mind. Basically, tension is the pull between the upper thread that comes through the eye of your needle and the bobbin thread. It is like a little tug-of-war. In machine embroidery, you want the bobbin thread to win. You want the bobbin thread to be able to pull just a little of the top thread to the back of your work, but not so tightly that your fabric puckers or distorts.

You will need to know how to adjust the tension on your machine. Check your manual. Your upper thread travels between the tension discs. These discs are controlled by the tension settings. A higher tension setting (higher number) sets the discs closer together leaving a narrower pass for the thread to travel through. The thread goes through more slowly and is held more tightly between the discs. Conversely, when you lower the tension setting (lower number) the discs open allowing the thread to flow more freely.

When you use a heavy thread like 12-weight cotton, you will want to lower the tension (open up the discs) so that the thread will move freely. Likewise, a flat metallic thread requires a lower tension that allows the thread to flow freely through the discs and not floss itself in the pathway. On the other hand, when you use a 40-weight rayon thread (which is much lighter than regular sewing thread) you will need to tighten the tension to a higher number so that the tension discs hug the thread. Otherwise, it will have too much free flow.

The weight and thickness of the bobbin thread will also affect tension. For thread painting, always use a bobbin thread that is lighter weight than the top thread. If the bobbin thread is too heavy, it will add too much bulk to the back of the work, which distorts and causes nests of knots. When using a 40-weight rayon thread for embroidery, use a 60-weight lightweight bobbin thread made for machine embroidery. When using a 35-weight cotton thread in the needle for thread painting, use regular 50-weight sewing thread in the bobbin. Cotton texture in the bobbin thread will grab the needle thread and hold it in place. The pre-wound bobbins don't work well with thread painting. They are wound too tightly and some of them are too slick. Try to work with compatible threads before changing the tension settings too much. If you are lowering the upper tension too much, then try to get a thicker bobbin thread.

Buy a second bobbin case. When you buy your machine, the bobbin tension is set by the company to maximize the tension settings of the machine. This is especially important if you have a computer sewing machine. Once you change the tension on the bobbin case, you will never get it back to the original tension and it won't work well with the programmed stitches and embroidery. If you want to monkey with the tension of the bobbin case, buy a second one.

Even the needle you choose can affect the tension. If the eye of the needle is too small for the thread, the thread has to work too hard going through. It may fray or break.

The fabric and stabilizer should support the thread. Big stitches with heavy threads won't work really well with tightly woven or flimsy fabric. Polyester fabric will deflect the needle resulting in skipped stitches. Lots of small tight stitches on a heavy fabric will get lost in the nap and pucker the fabric.

Three extremely important tension factors: user/operator/YOU. When you work with your sewing machine, do you pull and tug at your fabric trying to speed things up? Do you sew really fast and then stop on a dime? These things affect the tension of the thread. When you pull at the fabric, you don't give the machine a chance to finish the stitch and it distorts. If you hit the gas and try to stop on a dime, your needle thread still has momentum and can jump out of tension. When you are sewing around a curve, you need to sew a little slower, because you are covering more ground and the bobbin thread will pull tighter. It's just like driving a car; slow down before you stop and take the curves slowly.

Experiment with each new type of thread to find the best combination of settings, bobbin thread, needle, fabric, and stabilizer. Your experience will be your best resource. When you find a good combination, write the information on the test sample and keep it. A ringed binder with plastic page protectors is a good way to create your own thread-painting reference book.

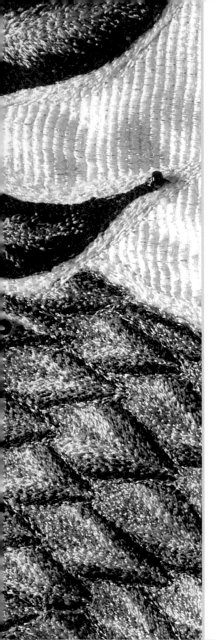

FABRICS: DO I HAVE TO CHOOSE JUST ONE?

It goes without saying that the fabric you choose will determine the finished look of your project. As you can see throughout this book, the variety of results is nearly endless. The only real way to know if a fabric is suitable for the look you are after is to test the fabric beforehand.

A test sample is only valid when you use the same materials and techniques as you will use in the finished piece. If you will be stitching densely on the fabric, stitch a dense design to test it. If you will be thread-drawing, stitch an open design on a test sample. Use the very same threads, fabrics, stabilizer, needle, machine, and techniques for your test sample.

If you are new to thread painting, use 100 percent cotton fabric. It is the easiest fabric to use. It has give, accepts stitches readily, and is stable.

Muslin is always a good choice. Without a print or color to distract, you can see exactly what you are doing. Don't use the lowest quality muslin called utility muslin. It shows the spaces between the woven threads. Use the next best quality—ordinary muslin. It may be labeled as permanent press, which is fine so long as it contains no polyester. It is usually a couple of bucks a yard. Avoid the high thread count muslin, which will distort your many stitches.

The body of *Thar Be Dragons Here* uses a fabric that mixes lamé, nylon, and acetate! This beautiful novelty fabric shouldn't be ironed. Also, it badly frays. The separate design elements were stitched on muslin and then applied to the fabric.

When thread painting a solid appliqué that will be sewn to another fabric, use regular muslin or colored 100 percent cotton for the foundation. It gives the best control and it won't break apart with the many stitches you make. You can easily draw the design onto the fabric. It is stable and holds its tension in the hoop without distortion.

Quilt-weight cotton fabric comes in just about every color and texture anyone could ever want. Personally, I love using beautiful, artisan hand-dyed fabrics. I just think they're the greatest ever. Check out your local quilt shops and quilt shows for the best quality and variety of fabrics.

My Big Fat Greek Still Life was total fun start to finish. It began with a beautiful hand-dyed fabric that I purchased at a quilt show. The still life was thread painted. The remainder of the design was "thread drawn." I felt like the fabric was just too good to cover up entirely, so I left the work looking like an unfinished painting. I love the effect and plan to do it again.

Drapery or dress linen fabrics have a thick and open weave that allows them to wonderfully accept stitches. Use 35-weight cotton threads and big stitches on this fabric for a crewel embroidery effect. Make a large design with little or no tiny details. This fabric is also wonderful for doing open decorative work. Any kind of thread can be used.

Osnaburg gives you a similar effect as linen. It is sort of a cross between muslin and linen. You can usually find it near the muslin in the fabric store.

If you are new to thread painting, avoid densely woven, high thread count fabrics.

Some batiks have high thread counts and contain a residual wax left over from the dying process. These fabrics have less "give." **Silk habitae** is very tough to stitch through.

Polyester deflects stitches causing skipped stitches. Nylon, all I can say is ouch!

I am not saying you should never use these fabrics. Just don't begin your learning process with them. Once you've got the hang of things, try everything.

WHICH BRINGS US TO THE NEXT LESSON—TRY EVERYTHING!

Ideas Take Shape (details). *This abstract embroidered panel was stitched with a variety of WonderFil® threads on drapery linen.*

Thread Painting MADE EASY ~ TERRY WHITE

Wonderful effects can be achieved with unusual fabrics. Felted wool, sheer overlays, gold netting, water-soluble stabilizer, even high rag content paper can be thread painted with wonderful results. I love to experiment with upholstery fabrics, dress wools, coat wools, lamé, raw silk, silk, and cotton organdy.

When you experiment with these fabrics, you will find that certain threads work best with each type of fabric, though you may need to change the needle and further adjust tensions. This is why testing your combinations is so important. The same needle and thread will not work the same on all fabrics.

For example:

When stitching on a fine organdy, use 40-weight rayon threads and a 75 needle. On heavy linen, using a 12-weight cotton with a denim needle gives a crewel embroidery effect. On densely woven fabrics or batiks, use a Microtex needle.

I keep a notebook of experiments. I put the sample test and notes in a clear page protector. This way, I can refer to good tests and "bad" ones later when I'm getting ready for a new project. After all, it could be that a "bad" test gives you the exact look you are going for.

Prewash your fabrics. A quilt-weight cotton fabric may perfect before it's washed, only to find out that the desired body that made the fabric perfect was just laundered away. Not washing your fabrics at all can leave finishing chemicals on your materials which can result in an allergic reaction. Also, the fabric's finish may deflect the needle, causing skipped stitches. Once in a while, a colorfast fabric may not be so colorfast. Shrinkage may also occur.

FINDING THE RIGHT STABILIZER

Always use a stabilizer in your work when you want to prevent distortion of the fabric. If you want to artistically distort the fabric with stitches, then a stabilizer may not be necessary.

After years of experimentation, I have found that there is no one perfect stabilizer for everything. That's why there are so many on the market.

A stabilizer is anything that will stabilize your fabric so that it will receive and hold stitches well. The nature of any type of embroidery is to distort the fabric and this is especially true of thread painting.

A stabilizer can be a woven fabric or interfacing, a non-woven interfacing, a stabilizer made for machine embroidery, or a knitted interfacing made to give and move with clothing.

Woven stabilizer

A woven stabilizer is good when stitching on a fabric that is loosely woven, bonded (felt, for example), or knitted. It will serve to control these unruly fabrics by adding a structure to hold the stitches in place. Cotton fabrics (such as muslin, organdy, and Osnaburg), lightweight linen, or a woven interfacing are all good choices. Just keep in mind that the woven fabric must be thick enough to keep the bobbin thread from coming up to the top. Also, the weave must open enough to receive the stitches.

Non-woven stable interfacing

Use non-woven stable interfacing with woven fabrics such as muslin, linen, and quilt-weight cotton fabrics. This type of interfacing has little give and won't interfere with the weave of a fabric. I often use two layers of a lightweight interfacing for added thickness to keep the bobbin thread from coming up to the top. Even the inexpensive interfacings work well; however, be sure to test their reaction to a hot iron before using them.

Stabilizers made for machine embroidery

There are so many specialty stabilizers on the market for machine embroidery. The manufacturers have guides for all of their specific uses and specialty techniques. Have some fun exploring all these possibilities. Test out all of the various uses and see how they enhance your work. Specialty stabilizers can be expensive if you do a lot of thread painting, but they're a lot of fun to work with. Personally, I love the water soluble ones.

Jazz Cat Jacket is made of silk linen. The cat and blue notes were stitched separately on muslin and then appliquéd. The lines of sound were stitched directly onto the jacket. Knit tricot interfacing stabilizes the jacket and keeps its shape.

Thread Painting MADE EASY ~ **TERRY WHITE**

People ask me if I use the specialty tearaway stabilizer. I used to use them all of the time. Now, I use them some of the time whenever I want to tear away the stabilizer. More often, however, I want a stabilizer that will stay in the work and keep it stable after the work is done.

Knitted Interfacing

The knitted tricot interfacing is great when doing open stitching on clothing. This lightweight stabilizer stays in the work (it is not removed after stitching), which helps to prevent distortion. It is lightweight, so it won't stiffen the garment. Also, it works as your interfacing as well as a stabilizer. It is especially wonderful for quilt tops with open stitching because it is easy to quilt through. Be careful about the hot iron.

The important thing is to use a stabilizer. Many different stabilizers will work for any given project. My best advice is to test the stabilizer with your materials.

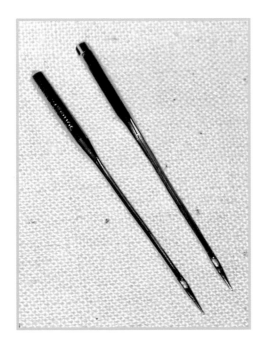

KNOW YOUR NEEDLES

Choosing the proper needle will depend on the threads and fabric used in your project. The needles I suggest throughout the book are for specific lessons. Like everything else, it's best to try out materials and techniques beforehand to ensure a great result.

In most cases, the best needle to use is a 90/14 embroidery needle. Its sharp point cleanly pierces most fabrics and doesn't skip stitches. When stitching densely, the point must continue to pierce through an increasing number of stitches. If a ball point needle is used, eventually, the needle will push the work into the hole in the needle plate and make a mess. The 90/14 has a large eye that allows thread to easily pass while stitching, which prevents tension problems. It has a deep groove on the front of the needle, which partially encloses the thread preventing frays and breakage.

There is no need to worry that the "big holes" created by the needle will be evident. The natural fiber fabrics will relax around the threads after stitching.

A Metallica needle is great for metallic threads. It has a bigger eye, deeper front groove, and a coating that helps reduce friction with the novelty threads.

100 Topstitch or Denim needles are the big guns appropriate for the heaviest threads on thick or rough fabric.

The Microtex needle helps when stitching on tightly woven fabrics, micro fibers, and batiks.

THREADS: OUR SEEMINGLY ENDLESS PALETTE

What can I say about the wonderful thread companies who have given us so many beautiful threads to work with? Thank you!

The sight of threads can inspire the same creativity in all of us that Picasso must have felt at his local paint shop. The weights and content of threads can also overwhelm us if we aren't sure how to use them. Thread manufacturers have great information about their own threads. In the Resource section of this book, there are references to several helpful Web sites. There is a great document called "A Thread of Truth" put out by YLI right on their Web site. It contains almost all the technical information you would ever want to know about threads.

The various companies market threads for specific uses, that is, machine quilting or embroidery. Don't be thrown off by a name. If it is beautiful and it is what you are looking for, stitch with it.

If you have a problem with breakage of threads, pay attention to where the break is occurring. Look to see if the thread is getting hung up on the edge of its own spool. If the thread breaks in the tension discs, then that is where an adjustment needs to be made. It may have to be rethreaded or the discs opened up a little more (lower the tension). If your thread is breaking at the needle, it could be the needle or the fabric that is causing the problem. You may need a larger needle

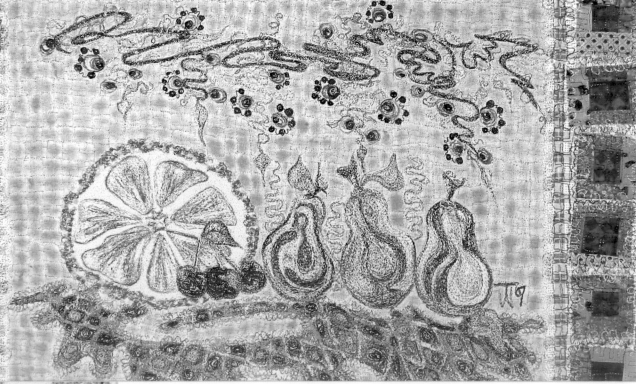

to protect the thread. It could be that you are trying to stitch through fabrics fused with a heavy fusible web and the stiffness is fraying the thread.

On very rare occasions, a thread just won't work. If it frays and breaks too much, you can just imagine how long it will hold up in your finished work. Don't use it. It could just come from a bad batch or it could be old and dry-rotted. This has happened to me about three times in the thousands of hours and threads I've used over the years.

Can you mix the different types and brands of threads in one project? **You Betcha!** Use the thread that is going to give you the aesthetic you are looking for. Treat each new thread as a scientific experiment. Stitch the thread on muslin to first understand its properties. Change one variable at a time. Try stitching it out on different types of fabric. Experiment with sheer overlays, appliqué, metallic, nubby, and wool fabrics. Wonderful effects can be achieved stitching on wool felt, upholstery fabrics, and hand-dyed fabrics.

The thickness of a thread is indicated on the packaging in terms of a number indicating its "weight." The lower the number, the thicker the thread: 60 weight is very fine and 30 weight is thick.

Keep in mind that this discussion of threads is based on what I know from my own experience only. Thread painting is not the same as other techniques and it is not the same as computer-generated embroidery. The information in this book applies to the techniques presented. So, if any of this is contrary to what others have told you in shops or a class, it's likely that that their techniques and results are different from mine. You may use different combinations of materials, needles, set-up, and techniques than those presented in this book and have great results, because every person and machine is different.

Rayon machine embroidery thread is available practically everywhere. This thread is made for the domestic embroidery machines. It is shiny, smooth, and looks like silk. Literally hundreds of colors are available. For years this was the only type of thread available to me. I learned to thread paint with it.

40-weight thread is very good for small designs and details in a picture. Use this thread when stitching intricate background designs or filling in areas with open stitching. The individual stitches will be more defined with the thinner thread as opposed to a thicker thread.

If you have lots of this thread and you want better coverage, use two threads through the eye of the needle. Thread your sewing machine the way you would for a twin needle and then thread them through the eye of your 90/14 embroidery needle.

You can also use these threads to create color blending and interesting mixes when using two at a time. If you don't have just the right color you can mix two colors that are similar in value and hue to get what you want. For example, you might mix a dark blue with a dark purple. The result is an almost iridescent effect of a color you might call midnight violet. Mixing colors like this increases your palette infinitely.

To tone down the color changes in a variegated thread, mix it with a solid color thread. Use two variegated threads at the same time for a mottled change of colors.

OPPOSITE: *Party of Pears*, 24" x 18", (detail). FROM THE COLLECTION OF WONDERFIL THREADS

When choosing a thread for each project, keep in mind that rayon thread will eventually fade. It cannot withstand rough wear. Occasionally, a deep red, navy, or black may run when laundered. If you intend to wash the finished project, test the thread for color bleeding. The finished design may be hand soaked in cold water and air dried. I say again, test the threads for colorfastness. You don't want your clown's red nose to bleed like mine did.

35- and 30-weight rayon threads are thicker and have more coverage than the 40-weight threads, but there are fewer colors available in these weights.

Variegated rayon machine embroidery thread comes in 40, 35, and 30 weights. Variegated threads change color as they progress, though the changes are different from brand to brand. A favorite thread of mine has three consistent color changes approximately every 7 inches. After stitching with a variegate for a while, you will begin anticipating when the color changes, which allows you to use it to great effect. For instance, you can stitch in one area at a time, concentrating each color in an area, or you can stitch all over for a mottled effect.

Twisted rayon machine embroidery thread consists of two different colors of thread twisted consistently through the spool. This thread seems softer than other rayon threads. Very interesting effects can be achieved with this thread.

Cotton machine embroidery thread can be found everywhere and in a horde of yummy colors, I might add. The beautiful matte finish on these threads looks unbelievably natural. A 40-weight cotton thread has more bulk than a 40-weight rayon thread, so it covers much like a 30-weight rayon thread.

Because they are cotton, these threads tend to fuzz up more than the rayon threads. Be sure to clean out the bobbin case area of your sewing machine often. Personally, I clean mine out each time I run out of bobbin thread.

These threads may fray more than others because of their fuzziness. Use a 90/14 embroidery needle or 100 topstitch needle. Open your tension discs a little bit more. When the thread breaks, rethread and keep on going. Beautiful results are well worth a little breakage.

That said, thread companies are improving the quality of these threads all the time. For instance, the Wonderfil Company makes Silco, which leaves very, very little fuzz.

Thread Painting MADE EASY ~ TERRY WHITE

Variegated cotton machine embroidery thread is made by several companies. I've included a list of the differences among the brands.

The color mix varies for thread to thread. Some have different shades of one color and some have an entire color family (yellow, pink, orange). Others might have completely different colors (red, green, gold). Some will even blend colors to surprising results (turquoise, green, blue and surprise! warm yellow).

The length of color change: Some threads change color in consistent lengths (i.e., every 2 inches); some threads change color in random lengths; some change in short lengths and some in longer lengths.

Consistency of color changes: Some have random color changes (colors are not in the same order); some have the same five colors repeated in the same order.

Thickness of the thread: They can be from 12 weight to 50 weight.

Finish of the thread: Some threads have a shiny appearance and some have a duller finish.

Cotton machine quilting threads are typically very strong and have a good tight twist, which helps reduce the fraying commonly associated with cotton embroidery threads. I think thread companies should rename them "Wonderful multi-purpose glorious threads that come in the best colors and on big spools." Because of their wonderful colors and variegates, I love thread painting with these.

Polyester threads are perfect for computer-generated machine embroidery and machine quilting. They can be used in thread painting; however, I find that these threads don't behave as well as natural fibers. They want to lie on top of the fabric's surface rather than cozying up to the other fibers, which prevents the threads from blending readily.

After saying all that, however, I need to qualify it. I use polyester threads in thread painting, but I don't suggest using them as a beginner. They behave a little differently than natural fibers while thread painting. Usually, the tension needs to be a little tighter when stitching with polyester.

I prefer to use a 75 or 80 needle with them. Because they are colorfast, the threads retain their vibrancy. Use these threads for strong graphic effects where blending will not be used or in projects that will get a lot of wear, such as handbags or outerwear.

Wrapped metallic machine embroidery thread starts with a strong polyester core that has shiny filaments twisted around the core. Be careful. These are somewhat fragile threads. Each company's brand is made differently and as such behaves differently.

Flat metallic machine embroidery thread is, just as the name implies, made from strands of flat coated metal alloy. These threads have a reputation for being the most difficult to work with, but the incredibly glittery effects are worth the trouble. To understand these threads, you will have to play around with them.

Bobbin thread is the thread that goes in the bobbin. Some threads are specifically made for machine embroidery work; rayon machine embroidery threads in 40, 35, and 30 weight and the metallic threads will work especially well with these. They include WonderFil® Deco-bob thread, YLI Soft Touch, Sulky® bobbin thread, and OESD.

In my experience, the prewound bobbin threads don't work well at all. They are wound too tightly, which affects the tension. My experience has shown that slick bobbin threads don't work well either. For thread painting you need a bobbin thread that grabs hold of the top thread. Instead, the slick bobbin thread seems to slip and slide when used with rayons and metallics.

For the heavier cotton threads use regular 50 weight cotton sewing thread or A&E® Maxi-Lock® serger thread. You need a heavier bobbin thread that can pull the top thread to the back of the work.

Novelty threads include every other thread not already listed. There are wooly threads, silk, linen, neon, glow-in-the dark, Japanese gold threads, etc. By all means, experiment with these things. Just do it after you know how to thread paint with the standards.

Some threads don't work well with the technique. Threads that are too thick or have a waxy finish or are very delicate don't stitch well. Use these threads for bobbin work or couch them to the work. There are great techniques for using all kinds of threads and yarns.

With the amazing differences in all the types and colors of threads from the various companies,

it is understandable that we would want to own **ALL** of them. I know—I'm working on it. When you come upon a new thread, buy at least four colors such as red, blue, yellow and green. That way you can thread paint a picture with them to see how it behaves. If you like it—**BUY MORE!**

THE STITCHES

When I began to experiment with thread painting, I would hoop a blank piece of fabric and just stitch textures and lines. My big learning step came once I put a picture on the fabric. All of a sudden, I had something to shoot for. Working on a leaf, I could develop shading and textures specific to a leaf. Working on an animal, I figured out the different stitches (and threads) needed to create fur or a shiny eyeball. I found that stitching on pictures was the key to learning and developing my stitch vocabulary.

Everyone stitches differently. Your physical motion is unique to you, just like your signature. Some people like to use large motions and make large pictures, others like things small and precise. Then there is everyone in between.

The stitches shown here are the ones I've identified in my work. The fun is in experimentation and finding new stitches to express what we see. This list is just the beginning.

We will use the stitches described here. They will be referenced by name throughout the book. The photos that illustrate the stitches are approximated actual sizes. The stitches have been made with various types of thread and in different sizes and aspects to show the many effects you can achieve with just one stitch.

All of these stitches were made with the straight stitch setting on the sewing machine.

Many people ask me why I don't use the zigzag stitch on the sewing machine. First, the zigzag stitch has a built-in distortion problem. With a straight stitch I have more freedom to create all the stitches you see here. Last but not least, my needle would break on my single stitch needle plate.

A Note on Underlay Stitching. Even after five years of thread painting, I continued to struggle with distortion problems. I had been thread painting for about five years and one of the problems I struggled with was distortion. I tried many stabilizers, different fabrics, conversations and e-mails with other textile artists. Still I had puckering whenever I stitched densely in one direction.

Being a thread painter, textile artist (and a snob), I would not even look at an embroidery machine or watch it work—until one day I did. That smart embroidery machine was laying down stitches perpendicular to the dense directional stitching that was used to create the design. The added stabilization of these underlay stitches made all the difference in the world to my thread painting.

To underlay, lay down stitches in a zigzag manner moving the fabric back and forth before stitching in an area with a dense directional stitch. The underlay is usually perpendicular to the final stitches. This helps to prevent distortion of the fabric.

Generally, use the thread that you are stitching with for the underlay in each area. If the thread is heavy, you might consider using a lighter weight thread that is the color of the fabric. Underlaying with a heavy thread can show through the stitching as bumps. I would not suggest using a clear thread as an underlay because if it shows through, it will shine like a metallic thread.

Thread Painting MADE EASY ~ **TERRY WHITE**

Glossary of Stitches

BUTTONHOLE OR BLANKET STITCH – Stitch several stitches straight, then stitch perpendicular for several stitches, then backstitch to the main stitch line, and repeat. The advantage of a free-motion buttonhole (this stitch made large is called a blanket stitch) is the freedom of the stitch size. It is also a great stitch for appliqué.

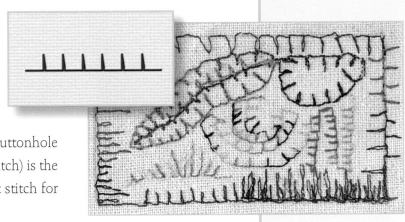

CHAIN STITCH – Stitch overlapping elongated loops in a row. This stitch can mimic crocheted lace.

CHEVRON STITCH – Stack rows of stitched Vs. When stitching the rows side by side, the next row can be stitched upside down for a different effect. This stitch is most effective when made with variegated threads. It creates great bird feathers and sheaves of wheat. No underlay is needed.

CIRCULAR STITCH – Stitch small overlapping circles. Varying the size of the circles changes the texture. Small round circles give a much different effect than long oval Os. This is a good texture for citrus fruit, wooly lambs, or a great background texture. No underlay is needed.

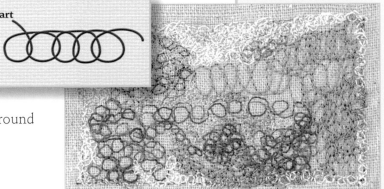

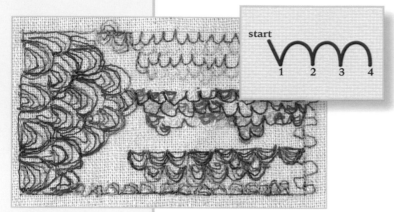

CLAM SHELL STITCH – Rows of half circles are stitched. Great for fish scales, clouds, the roof of a house.

CONTOUR STITCH – Smooth lines stitched side by side are used to fill in an area. The direction and shape of the lines mimic the contours of the shape to be filled. When filling an area, an underlay stitch should be used to avoid distortion. The partially finished apple in the photo shows the underlay stitch.

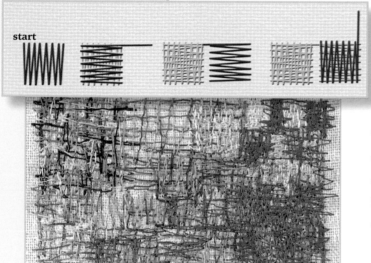

CROSSHATCH STITCH – Stitch big zigzags up and down and then cross with big zigzags back and forth to create a square shape. This is one of my favorite background textures. This stitch has its own underlay stitch.

FRENCH KNOT – This is a very tight and overstitched spiral stitch. It can be done individually or in clusters. When stitching individual knots, you can travel to the next point on the fabric by using serpentine stitches or jump stitches. Jump stitches can be cut or, as in the photo, used as part of the design. No underlay is needed.

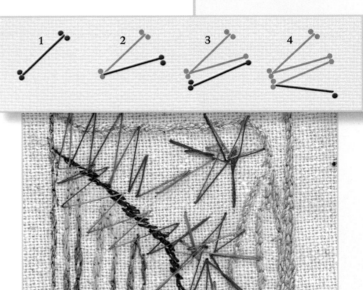

JUMP STITCH – Put the needle in and out of the fabric and take a tiny stitch in the same place to anchor the thread, then raise the presser foot. Move the needle to another point on the fabric and put the needle in and out a few times to anchor the thread. This creates a very long stitch that is great for whiskers on a kitten or a flower's stamen. No underlay is needed.

This stitch is also created when moving the needle at the finish of one area of stitching to the beginning of another area (as shown with the French knots and seed stitch). These threads can be cut or left as part of the design.

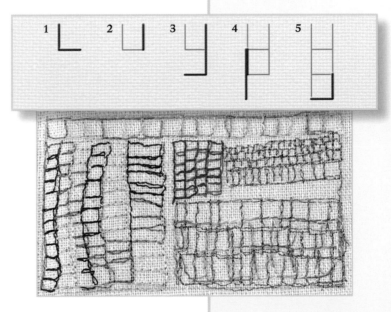

LADDER STITCH – Stitch a row of buttonhole stitches, then close them with a line of stitching to create boxes. This is a great stitch for decoration and patterning.

LAZY DAISY – Stitch loops in a circle. No underlay is needed.

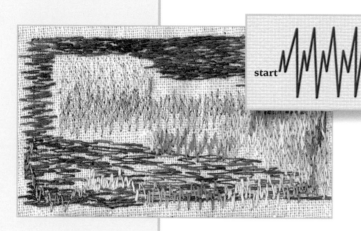

LONG AND SHORT STITCH – Create these by zigzagging your needle in random lengths. Stitches should be close together. The second row of stitches should be the same as the first, etc. This stitch is used to blend colors in a fill area. The rough texture is effective for animal fur. Used in a landscape, it creates lovely grass fields. When stitching densely in one direction, this stitch requires an underlay stitch.

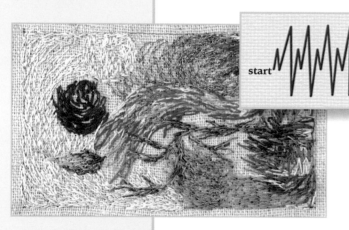

LONG & SHORT CONTOUR STITCH – This stitch is wonderful for filling in when a rough texture is required. The long and short stitch has less distortion than the smooth contour stitch because the lines are broken up. The long and short stitch can be used along the curve of a design.

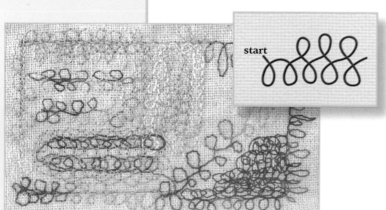

LOOP STITCH – This can be used with the circular and serpentine stitches to create interesting textures. No underlay is needed.

OUTLINE STITCH — Create a smooth single line of stitching for drawing, detailing, and outlining. The same stitch is used for free-motion quilting. No underlay is needed.

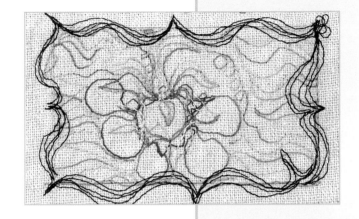

OVERSTITCH — This is used to build up an area with layers of color to create extra depth and complexity of design. When I intend to overstitch, I stitch all the layers with open stitches so that all the colors can be seen. An overstitch can sometimes consist of a detail stitched with a contrasting thread over existing stitching. Too much overstitching can cause thread tension problems.

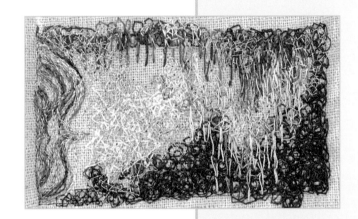

RUFFLE STITCH — Very similar to a serpentine stitch, though the ruffle stitch has extra stitching along one curve. This is a great stitch for many designs, especially eddies in a stream, decoration on clothing, and border designs.

SATIN STITCH (NON-PADDED) — Thread is laid from one side of the area to the other by putting the needle in and out on one side; then needle in and out on the other. Stitches lie close together for a solid fill. It takes some practice when filling in a large area. Stitch underlay is perpendicular to the final stitches.

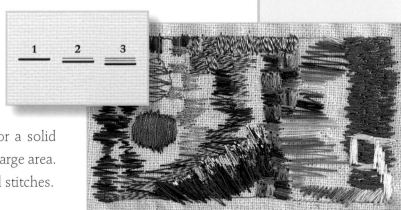

SATIN STITCH (PADDED) – A dense underlay is stitched first. Then the satin stitch is made over it. This creates a raised effect, as illustrated in the photo by the purple circle.

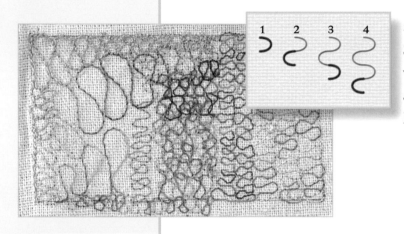

SEED STITCH – Outline an oval shape. Fill in with several rows of long stitches, then outline stitch with several rows of stitching. Raise the needle and move to another area to make another stitch. This makes a connection of one stitch to the next with a single thread (known as a Jump Stitch). Jump stitches can be used as part of the design, or they can be cut. No underlay is needed.

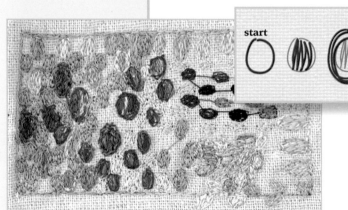

SERPENTINE STITCH – Stitch connected Ss. This can be a lovely fill-in stitch. It is used with the circular stitch fill, or for when you are stitching in a tight spot. It also creates lace edging.

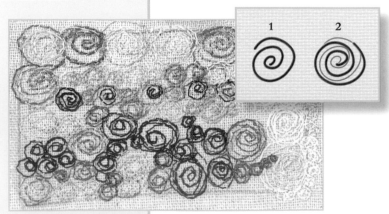

SPIRAL STITCH – Stitch the outline of a circle, and then spiral in and out. This stitch looks like bubbles and shells. It makes a great background stitch and border stitch.

STEM STITCH – A single line of stitching; make several stitches forward, then backstitch a few, then several stitches forward, backstitch a few, and so on. This creates a bolder stitch than an outline stitch. No underlay is needed.

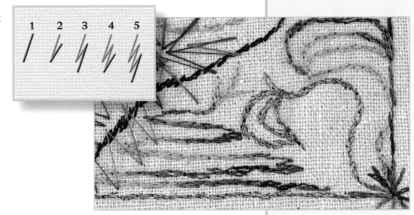

SQUARE STITCH – Stitch overlapping squares. This is a wonderful background texture stitch. It has its own underlay.

TRIANGLE STITCH – Stitch overlapping triangles. This is a great angular fill. It creates the stars we all drew as little kids and it has its own underlay.

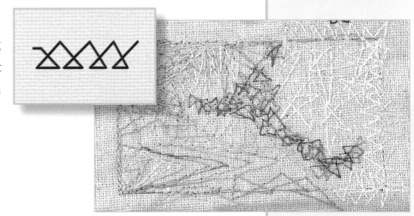

A companion video to the stitches is available. Check Resources on page 110 for information.

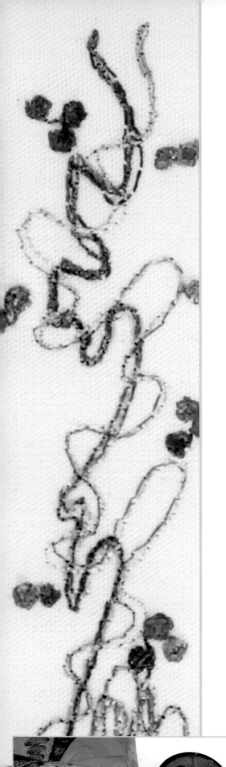

HOW TO THREAD PAINT

Start with a simple design drawn with a solid black line on white paper. Make several copies to experiment with different color combinations. Use colored pencils to shade in the drawing. This accomplishes two things. First, it establishes the colors beforehand so that time and thread aren't wasted. Also, the pencils marks will help to determine the type of stitches you will use. This process prepares you for stitching.

Trace the black outline of the drawing onto the same fabric you will be stitching. Use a very fine point archival pen. Pigma® Micron® pens are good for this. They are available at office supply stores.

Place the fabric onto the stabilizer. Hoop them together.

A good screw-type embroidery hoop is essential. I have found the best hoop: Morgan's No-Slip Hoop. A hoop will make the work easy to handle by giving you greater control of the work and helping to prevent distortion. The hoop should be gently guided (not gripped) under the needle. Unlike spring hoops, the No-slip Hoop will hold the fabric with even tension and will not slip. Craft hoops or other plastic hoops do not hold the fabric tight enough for thread painting.

Hoop the fabric and stabilizer with the larger ring on the bottom and the smaller ring on the top. It helps to stand up when you are doing this. If the depth of the no-slip hoop does not slide under your presser foot, take the presser foot off when positioning the hoop under the needle.

Place the hoop under the sewing machine needle. Position the needle at your starting point on the design. Holding onto the needle thread with your hand, insert the needle into the fabric, pull it up and draw the bobbin thread to the top of the work. Draw the top thread under the presser foot. While holding onto these two threads, take a few stitches. Cut the loose thread ends.

When stitching a design larger than the hoop, stitch the section in the hoop completely. Take the work out of the hoop, press the work upside down on a fluffy towel to iron out the hoop marks, and then hoop the next section.

Let's Stitch!

Important: Gently hold the edges of the hoop. Don't grab the hoop. If you do, your hands will be too tense to make smooth motions. **Don't press down on the hoop.** This causes friction against the machine bed, preventing smooth movements.

Very Important: Get the needle going before you move your hoop. Start your machine and then move your hoop with gentle swooping motions. It helps to stitch from side to side instead of back and forth. Otherwise, you won't be able to see what you're stitching.

You want to achieve a balance between the needle's speed and the speed of your hoop's movement. You will begin to develop a rhythm and feel the smooth motion when you get it just right. **The needle should be stitching at a medium speed.** If you stitch too slowly, you'll feel the friction between the needle and the fabric. You can bend or break a needle this way. Don't stitch fast either. It creates tension problems and will cause you to lose control. Think of riding a bike for the first time. If you go too slowly, you wobble. If you go too fast, you run off of the road.

Practice makes better.

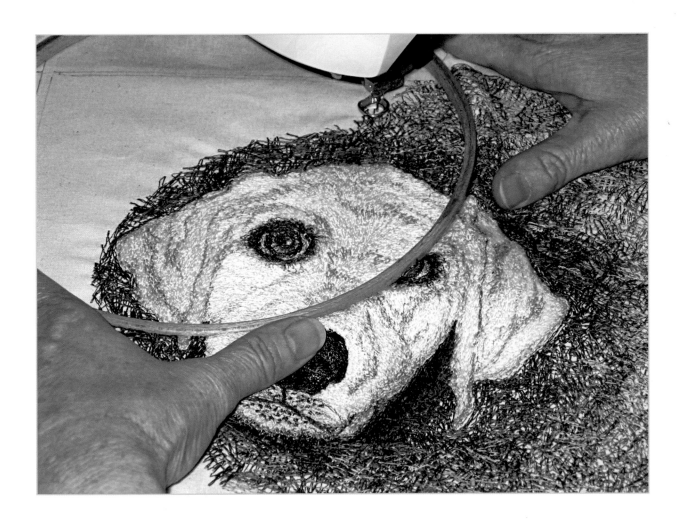

YOUR SEWING PERSONALITY

You can learn so much about a person just by watching her sew. Some people are impeccably precise and careful. Some grab the fabric and in a blink they are off to the races. (Okay, that is just tension problems waiting to happen!) Some people are tentative, afraid to make a mistake. Then there are those who are one with their machines. That is how we should all aspire to be.

I want to impress upon you the importance of striking a balance between the speed of your machine and the easy flow of the fabric underneath. Stitch size and good tension are controlled more by what you do than what the machine does. A happy balance will create beautiful stitch quality.

If the machine speed is too fast and the fabric moves too slowly, you will pull up bobbin thread, which leaves little dots rather than stitches. This often happens when someone is trying to get little, precise stitches. If this happens to you, just slow the speed of your machine for better control and beautiful, even stitches.

If you are pulling at the needle and can feel the needle strain against the fabric, thread tension problems will result. This happens when people are trying to make big, swooping stitches. Just speed the machine up a little. Stitching too slowly is like riding a bike too slowly; your stitches will be rickety and wobbly. Don't worry about staying in the lines. To achieve the rhythm you want, you just might have to practice swooping for awhile.

Lady Elizabeth, 35" x 43", (detail)

Thread Painting MADE EASY ~ TERRY WHITE

SECTION II
Lessons

Berry Fields, 51" x 37", (detail on pages 4–5). *The large fern was thread painted separately on cotton, then appliquéd to the pieced background. The rest of the images were thread painted directly on the patchwork. The berries were stitched together with free-motion stitching. The thread used is Superior King Tut™ cotton thread.*

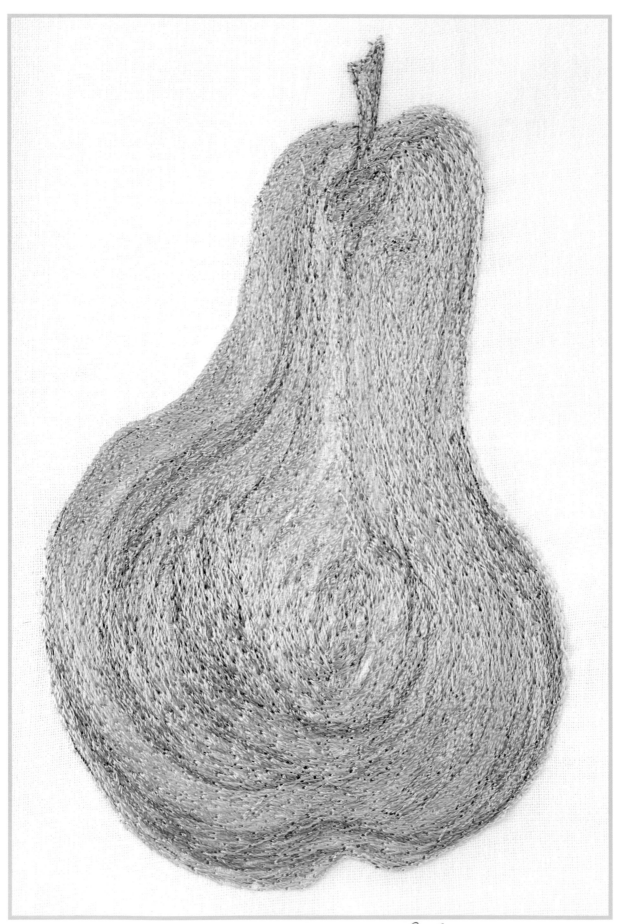

Thread Painting MADE EASY ~ **TERRY WHITE**

LESSON 1 ~ *The Pear*

We will start with a single shape design. *The Pear* demonstrates the effects you can achieve with only one type and weight of thread. With this easy, rounded design, focus on developing smooth movements. Note that the direction of the stitching is important, as is the application of the colors, which blend and shape the form.

First, trace the shape onto white paper. Use colored pencils to color in the shape using the kind of marks that you will make with your sewing machine. Match your threads to the colored pencils. This won't make for much of a surprise with your finished result; however, you can change the colors anytime you want. One of the "free" parts of free-motion embroidery means complete freedom to change colors at whim.

Trace the pear onto your muslin with a fine .01 Micron Pigma pen. The line should be clean, not sketchy. Don't worry. You'll cover the lines with your stitching and the pen will not bleed through your work. Keep in mind, these are "suggested lines to go by," not to "stay in."

Hoop your muslin with a lightweight, non-woven interfacing or stabilizer.

We will use 40-weight rayon threads in five colors: golden yellow, peach, marigold, pale green, and lilac.

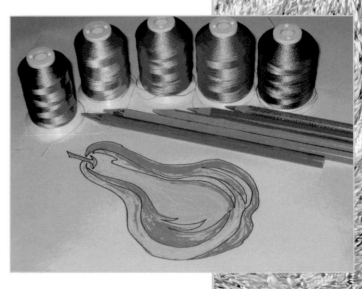

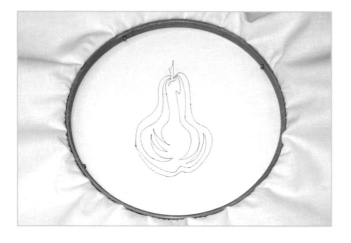

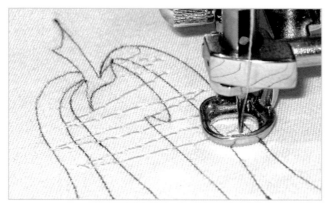

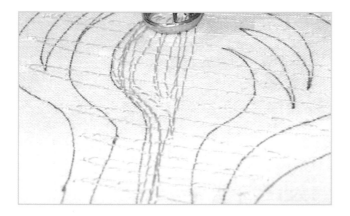

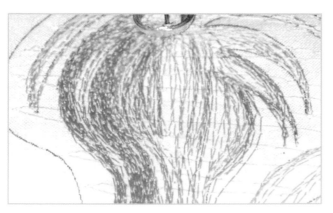

Let's Stitch!

We will start with the color yellow because it is the predominant color in the design. Second, we will stitch the marigold because it is closest in value and hue to the yellow. Blend as you stitch. Next we will stitch with peach, then lilac, and lastly green. Accent colors are saved for last because they are only lightly added for accent and contrast. If used too soon, they will be too heavily stitched in the design.

Underlay stitches are important to keep the work from distorting. Start with the main color, in this case yellow. Because it is such a light color, the yellow underlay stitches won't show through the stitching. **If there are many colors in a motif, use a thread that matches the fabric color for the underlay stitches.**

Where the stitches are long, they should be done in lengthy sweeps that follow the contours of the drawn lines. Some areas are stitched densely by sweeping back and forth. Some areas are stitched more openly to leave room for other colors. Try to avoid too much overstitching. It will create distortion and the stitching won't be as good. If you need to fill in an area, slow down and concentrate. Fill it in carefully. Free-motion work is not done at top speed.

Notice that I went "outside of the lines!" You can also see that the work is now upside down. Manipulate the hoop in any direction that makes it easier to see what you are doing. Move the hoop so that the presser foot doesn't hit the edge of the hoop. You may find it easier to see what you are doing by stitching side to side instead of back and forth.

 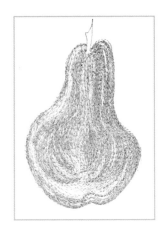  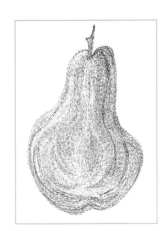

You can see that with the smooth contour stitching, the direction of the stitching is all-important. If you are very new to this kind of work, repeat this exercise until you are comfortable with your progress. Keep in mind that I worked at it for a year before I liked anything I did.

In the sequence of photos, you can see how colors were added. I didn't completely follow the colored picture, but using colored pencils first helped me to see where to stitch the colors in general. Notice how interesting the pear looks with just five colors. When the green is blended with yellow it looks different than when it is blended with the lilac. The more you work with different color combinations of thread, the more you can anticipate the effects you'll achieve.

STITCHING FOR CONTOUR SHAPE

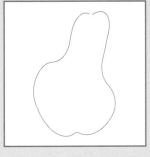

Draw the shape on fabric.

Underlay the stitches.

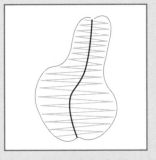

Bisect design with first line of stitches to establish form.

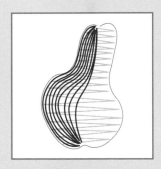

Stitch contour lines leaving areas unstitched to allow for color change.

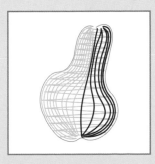

Stitch the other side of the shape.

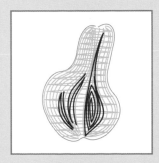

Fill in with other colors in empty spaces.

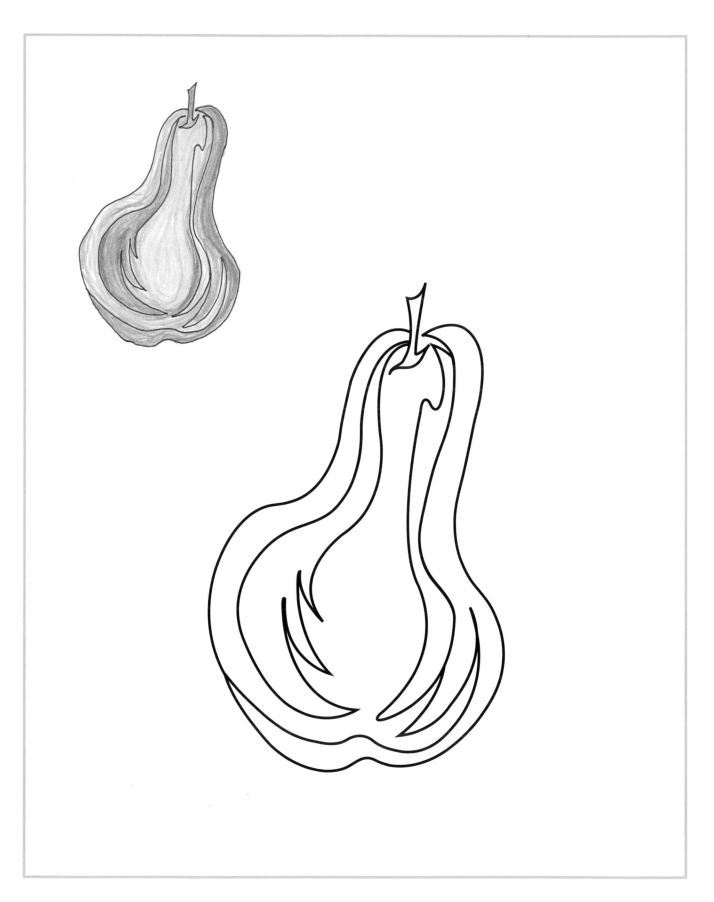

BLENDED COLORS: TWO THREADS AT ONCE

In this lesson, you will learn how to blend colors in a subtle way by threading two threads through your needle.

Two 40-weight rayon machine embroidery threads will easily stitch through the eye of a 90/14 machine embroidery needle. Thread your machine the way you would for a twin needle (check your sewing machine manual). If your machine has two pathways through the tension discs, use them. This will keep a consistent tension on each thread. If you have to run both threads through the tension discs in the same path, you may have to experiment with the tension setting to get consistent tensions on both threads. Sometimes, one thread will have less tension on it than the other. This may create an entirely new situation. I call it the "loop stitch." You just may enjoy the extra texture it provides to your work, or you may want to rethread and try again.

If you absolutely cannot thread both through your machine (I have never seen this happen on any machine), then stitch each thread one at a time. You will get a similar effect, though you'll have to stitch more openly. Also, the second color will be dominant unless you use the "twists" made by various thread companies.

Two threads provide good coverage in filled areas and create a bold stitching line.

When using two different colors of a similar hue and depth, the stitch will look iridescent. (Try dark blue and purple together—it's pretty). When using strong contrasting colors together, a "twist" look is created. If a dark and a light thread are used together, it may look as if bobbin thread is being pulled up. But maybe that's the look you want.

If one or both of the threads are variegated, a wonderful color mix can be achieved.

Two 40-weight threads threaded together create one heavy thread. Use regular polyester sewing thread in the bobbin for a good tension match. Use long stitches that give the thread mix a chance to show off.

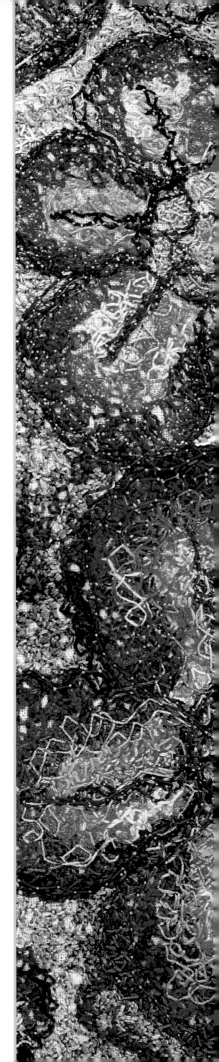

LESSON 2 ~ *Sun Spots*

Sun Spot I

40-weight rayon machine embroidery threads come in hundreds of luscious colors, but if the perfect shade still eludes you, use two at once to make a new mix. Your repertoire of threads has now multiplied to thousands of color possibilities. Yay!

Sun Spots originated from a group of drawings I made for some large thread paintings. This project teaches a subtle blending of two threads at a time through the eye of the needle. There are three designs in this lesson, each with a different degree of complexity. The first two are simplified versions of the third.

My Singer® Quantum® XL-6000 has a multifunctional thread delivery system. This thread exchanger is great for delivering two threads through the eye of the needle. Be sure to thread one color at a time with the automatic threading feature.

Materials:

THREADS USED

The threads are listed in the order of use.

1. **Light yellow** – Sulky 1067
2. **Warm yellow** – Sulky 1066
3. **Yellow orange** – Sulky 1024
4. **Orange** – Sulky 1065
5. **Dark orange** – Sulky 1184
6. **Fuchsia** – Sulky 1511

Fabric

12" square of Osnaburg fabric for each design

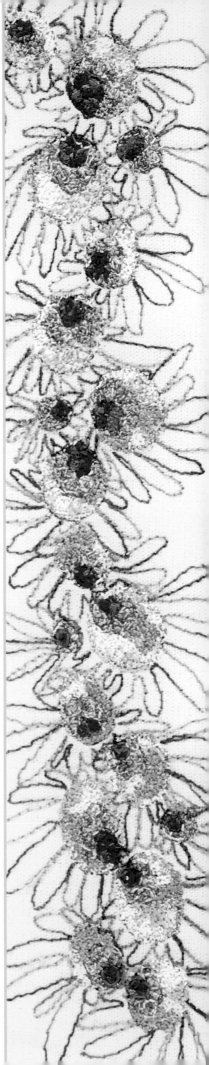

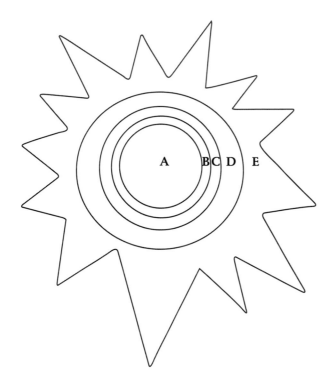

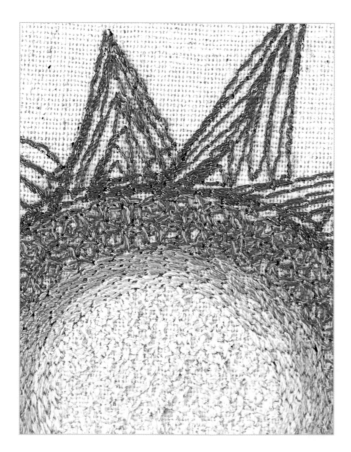

To begin, thread colors 1 and 2 through the eye of your needle. You may want to do a little sample stitching before beginning the design. The key is to adjust the machine to get good tension. Stitch in small circles and smooth, curved lines. When you are satisfied with the thread delivery, begin stitching the design.

Let's Stitch!

Start in the central circle of the sun (Area **A**). Stitch in open circles, overlapping some of the circles for extra texture.

Stitch Area **B** with colors **2** and **3**. Stitch along the contour of the shape using **long and short stitches**. Don't stitch around and around the design as if you were driving around a circle. It will create distortion. By filling in the area little by little, you can prevent that from happening.

Stitch Area **C** with colors **3** and **4**. Stitch in the same manner as Area **B**.

Stitch Area **D** with colors **4** and **5**. Stitch in the same circular manner as in Area **A**.

Stitch Area **E** with colors **5** and **6**. Stitch in **long contour stitches** following the lines of the sun rays. Start on the outside of each ray and stitch towards the center of the ray. Then using **long and short stitches**, outline the circle of the sun and cover the raggedy edges of each ray.

With this simple design, you have subtly blended threads, one color leading to the next, into a great rainbow effect.

A   B C   D   E

SUN SPOT II

Sun Spot II is slightly more complicated. The same color mixes are used, but in a different way. By using this color-mix method, the colors appear more integrated (like custom colors) and work perfectly side by side.

Let's Stitch!

Stitch Area **A** with colors **5** and **6**. Stitch in **open circular stitching**.

Stitch Area **B** with colors **4** and **5**. Stitch in **long and short stitches** along the contour of the circle.

Stitch Area **C** with colors **2** and **3**. Stitch in **long and short contour stitches.**

Stitch Area **D** with colors **3** and **4**. Stitch in **smooth contour stitches,** following the lines of the rays, starting from the outside of each shape and following towards the center.

Stitch Area **E** with colors **1** and **2** with **circular stitches**.

Stitch Area **F** with colors **4** and **5** with **smooth contour stitches.**

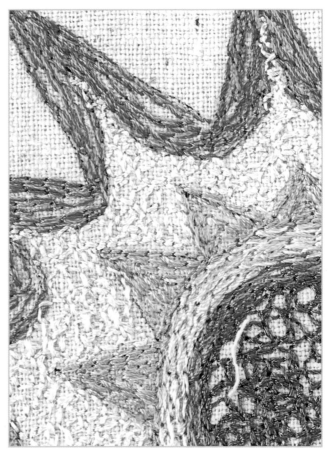

A BCD E F

LESSON 2~*Sun Spot-11*

Thread Painting MADE EASY ~ **TERRY WHITE**

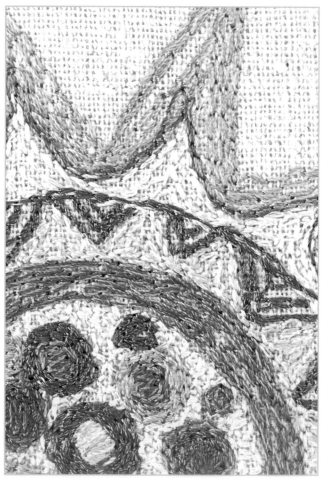

SUN SPOT III

Sun Spot III is the original design as I saw it in my head.

Let's Stitch!

There are sunspots in the center Area **A**. Each one is stitched in satin stitch with a different combination of threads. The rings around several of these spots are stitched in **long and short contour stitches**.

Stitch Area **A** background with colors **1** and **2** in **serpentine stitches**.

Stitch Area **B** with colors **3** and **4** in **long and short contour stitches** along the curve of the circle.

Stitch Area **C** with colors **2** and **3** in **smooth contour stitches**, following the lines of the rays.

Stitch Area **D** with colors **5** and **6** in **smooth contour stitches**, following the contours of the rays.

Stitch Area **E** with colors **1** and **2** in **smooth contour stitches**.

Stitch Area **F** with colors **3** and **4** in **smooth contour stitches**.

Stitch several rows of lines between Areas **E** and **F** with colors **4** and **5**.

The Ant Parade (detail) *is a design using Robison-Anton® rayon threads with twists of color, a particularly useful thread when only one thread is to be used to create many surprising effects. This design was thread painted onto a fabric painted with Tsukineko® dye paints. It was then machine quilted with a twist thread.* FROM THE COLLECTION OF GREG AND TAMMY FRASZ

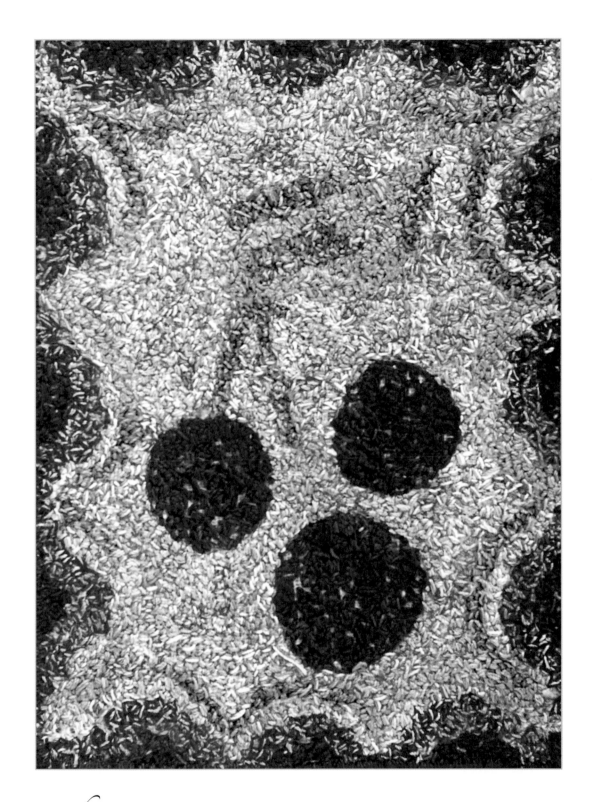

Cherry Rug, 3"x4", was stitched with two threads at a time using YLI cotton quilting variegated threads. It was made in such a way as to mimic Russian punch needlework. In the past, I have done punch work, so believe me when I say it takes a long while to complete a tiny project. This was stitched in less than two hours.

VARIEGATED COLOR THREADS ARE WONDERFUL THINGS

Variegated color threads are a little like chocolate. I could tell you how wonderful they are, but to appreciate them, you'll really have to try them for yourself.

Each variegated thread creates a unique effect with its stitch, which is why **I always experiment with every new thread before I use it in my work.** I test a multitude of stitches until I know how the thread's colors will blend and can anticipate where I might use the thread to its best effect.

When you are choosing your thread, be mindful that not all variegates are created equal. Lay the thread over a sheet of white paper to better see the colors, the length of the color changes, and the number of colors. Ask yourself, do the colors blend or do they contrast? Is there a random color change or are they in a consistent order? Are they different shades of one color or are they different colors?

Some variegates contain a very light, almost white color. If stitched on a white fabric, this will create an area void of color though with a texture. Depending on how it is used in the design, this can be either an unsettling or a really cool effect.

The thread collection of a single company will often repeat colors from one thread to another. This really helps with blending colors for certain effects.

The first variegated threads I used were the 30- and 40-weight rayon Sulky® threads. These change color about every 7 inches or so in a consistent pattern of three colors. After using them for a short time, I could anticipate their upcoming color change. For instance, if I wanted all the darker yellow to be in one area of my flower, I would stitch in that area until the color changed. I would stitch the second color in its own concentrated area and do likewise with the third color. When the darker yellow returned, I would "travel" with my needle back to the original spot. I could literally use three colors without having to thread my needle three times over.

Next, I experimented with the Oliver Twists threads by Jean Oliver. What yummy color combinations!

I must say, every variegated thread I have used, regardless of company, has been gorgeous. The designers and artists who mix these threads have an incredible color sense. I thank them all. It is a joy to work with these threads. They make my work all the better.

Thread Painting MADE EASY ~ **TERRY WHITE**

LESSON 3 ~ *Fruit Bowl*

In this lesson, you will create texture with varied stitches and color using variegated threads.

Three different brands of thread were used in *Fruit Bowl.* Each has its own unique characteristics. There are many great threads out there, but I chose to use these because I had them on hand. Believe me, I try every new thread as soon as possible. I have never met a thread I didn't like.

Materials

King Tut 40-weight thread by Superior has short intervals of beautiful colors. It is perfect for filling in areas with a mottled texture. Some of the color mixes have "surprises," i.e., colors you wouldn't expect to find mixed together. Experiment with these to see what the effects will be.

Blendables® 30-weight thread by Sulky have longer, random color intervals. This thread is good for contour stitching. It makes an interesting effect for drawing. Most Blendables are mixed shades of a single color. They are very useful whenever only one color is required.

Hand-dyed 35-weight variegates by Valdani have very long color intervals in gorgeous colors. The colors work with a variety of stitches to create a painterly effect. Sometimes the thread breaks. Just thread it up again.

If you have threads you'd prefer to substitute, use them.

Thread Painting MADE EASY ~ TERRY WHITE

THREADS USED

> Apple – Reds (King Tut 946)
>
> Orange and shine on the apple –
>   Orange/Yellow/Pink (Blendable 4003)
>
> Grapes – Purples (Valdani M25)
>
> Leaf – Greens (Blendable 4017)
>
> Tendrils and Green on the fruit –
>   Olives (Blendable 4019)
>
> Yellow details in the bowl – Yellows
>   (King Tut 985)
>
> Blue bowl – Blue/Violet (King Tut 903)
>
> Red ribbon and dots in bowl –
>   Red/Fuchsia/Orange (King Tut 914)

Let's Stitch!

Apple – Underlay stitches, and then **smooth contour stitch.** Stitch the shines in **contour stitching.**

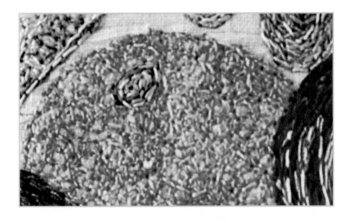

Orange – **Circular stitch.** No underlay stitching is needed because the circular stitching goes in all directions. Stitch in an open manner and then overstitch. This will break up the color better and give a more uniform mottled effect.

Grapes – **Smooth contour stitch.** Concentrate on one section of a grape. As the color changes, move to another section. When the color changes again, overstitch (just a little, just one or two lines of stitching), dark colors over a light area and light over a dark area. This creates areas of color in the grape instead of an allover mottled affect. No underlay stitching is necessary because the grapes are small.

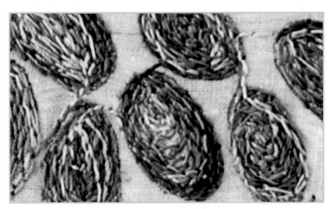

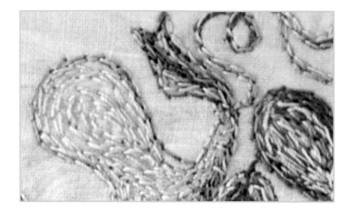

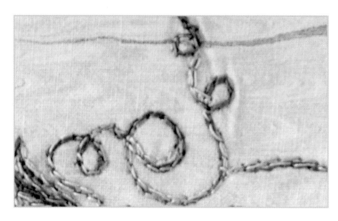

Leaf – **Open smooth contour stitch.** No underlay stitching is needed because the open stitching doesn't distort the fabric.

Edge of leaf – **Serpentine stitch** is used as an interesting detail.

Tendrils – **Stem stitch**

Blue bowl – **Long and short stitching** create a rough texture. Stitch horizontally along the rim of the bowl with long sweeping stitching. Use underlay stitches in the body of the bowl. Stitch a section at a time in a vertical manner. Open **serpentine stitch** the little square details on the rim. Outline the bowl in **stem stitch** for a smooth design.

Yellow detail on the bowl – **Smooth contour stitch** in a vertical direction to fill in the rim. Outline the rim areas with **long and short contour stitches.** Flower petals are filled with smooth contour stitches.

Red dot details on the bowl – **Padded satin stitch** and then **outline stitch.**

Ribbon – Use long, sweeping, open **smooth contour stitches.**

LESSON 3~ *Fruit Bowl*

Not So Still Life is one in a series of funny vases in a "moving" setting. This one is subtitled TAKE IT TO ROAD SHOW—IT'S GOTTA BE WORTH SOMETHING. This work was done entirely in YLI threads including rayon, polyester, and cotton solid and variegated threads. The matte cottons play off the shiny synthetic threads adding extra texture.

Stitch slowly and carefully when outlining in black. Use a 40-weight rayon or polyester thread for detailing tiny areas. The variegated charcoal/black thread used in this work seems to soften the line and add texture.

My Big Fat Greek Still Life (detail; full quilt shown on page 13) *used only Valdani 35-weight cotton variegated thread. The color changes in the thread are very long, perfect for large pieces. I left the thread-drawn background looking like an unfinished painting so as not to hide all of the beautiful hand-dyed fabric (which I think is perfect for this project). I couldn't be happier with the effect.*

The *Red Onion* is stitched in Valdani variegated threads on green fabric. The onion was cut and stitched by machine to the blue fabric you see. Then using a reverse-appliqué method, it was sewn back to the middle of the original green fabric using big hand-sewn stitches. The seeds are fused shapes. The piece is machine quilted.

Thread Painting MADE EASY ~ **TERRY WHITE**

The *Coleus* features a serpentine stitch used as an interesting detail along the edge of the leaf. The detail shows where channels of red fabric were left unstitched so it could be quilted between the shapes.

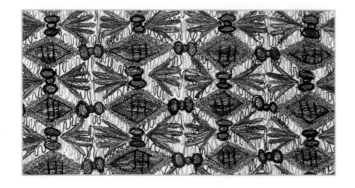

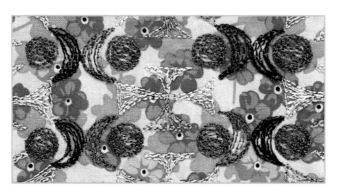

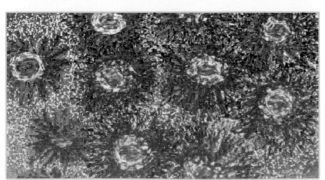

EXPERIMENT WITH PATTERN AND COLOR

Sometimes the sight of a perfect fabric will suggest a design or color combination. In the case of Gourdy, the Painted Bird, I already had a design, but the right color combination hadn't yet found me. When I stumbled upon this rosy tan color fabric from Cherrywood Fabrics, I knew it was perfect. The threads I laid onto the fabric were yummy! Gourdy was sprouting wings.

Keep in mind that when you are working with an allover pattern, the thread colors will seem to change. A color will appear different on a black background than a white or green background.

Make stitch samples to see which combinations of thread work best with your current project. For instance, I had to change several of the threads I originally chose. Regardless of its yummy factor, the blue was too pale. I chose a darker blue instead. The brown was too dull so it was exchanged for a terra cotta.

After your colors are finalized, test the type of stitches you will use. Stitch is equally as important as the colors chosen. Test the threads with the stitches on the same fabric you will be using in the project. Otherwise it won't be an accurate test. As you can see in the samples, the color and type of fabric used is also extremely important to the finished look.

You might find some stitches are not suitable for your current project. Save the stitch sample test in a page protector ringed binder for future reference. You never know when that stitch sample might come in handy.

LESSON 4~ *Gourdy*
the Painted Bird

Eight solid color 40-weight rayon machine-embroidery threads were used in this project:

Olive green

Sage green

Violet

Purple

Bright blue

Salmon

Dark brown

Maroon

This simple design is a starting point for experimentation. Rather than include the exact threads used, this is your opportunity to scour the shelves of your favorite stores. Because your fabric will be different, these colors will not necessarily fit your project

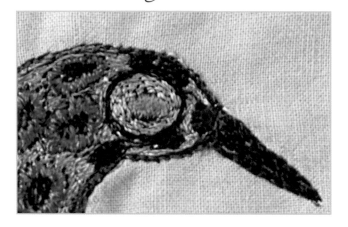

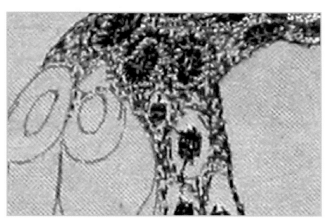

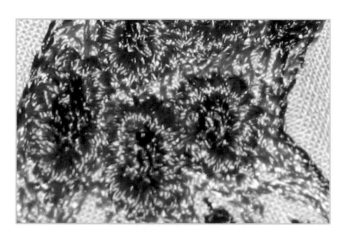

Let's Stitch!

Stitch the eye in the center with **olive green** using a **padded satin stitch. Sage green** is stitched around the eye in several rows of **outline stitch.**

The beak is stitched in **maroon** with **contour stitches.**

The front of the body is patterned. The **salmon** thread is used to **contour stitch** the background.

Next, make **dark brown seed stitches.** You can see the **jump stitches** which were cut before the next stitches were made.

Around each brown seed, make **satin stitches** with **bright blue** thread.

The same stitches are used on the top of the wings, though in different colors. **Violet** seeds are surrounded by **sage green satin stitches.**

The feathers on the sides of the wing are stitched with **olive green** and **purple.**

Shown below is the center row of feathers on the wing.

Scallop shapes are first stitched with **sage green,** using a **satin stitch,** then outlined. The shapes are filled in with **long and short stitches** in **violet.**

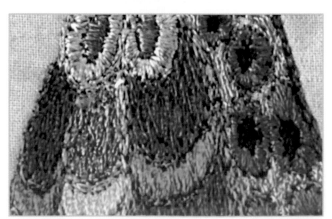

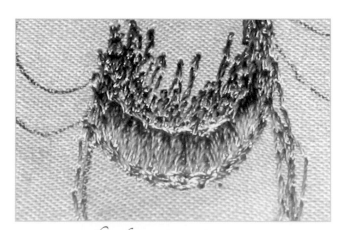

FASCINATION WITH COLOR

Color is our most powerful creative tool. Color is emotional, which explains why we are each uniquely drawn to certain color combinations. Through our art, we can constantly discover new things about the interaction of colors, as we begin to understand how they work. In fabric painting, colors are our voice.

There are scientific and psychological reasons as to why we are drawn to specific colors or color groups. Studies have been done! The list of factors is enormous and includes: the biological way our eyes and brain perceive color; the part of the world in which we live (city environment or country); the atmosphere and brightness of the sun where we live; the foliage surrounding us (or the lack of it); the colors in our own homes as we grew up and our emotional makeup. Think about that before the next time you say you're crazy for a color.

The essential thing is to be comfortable with our personal color choices. There are accepted color "rules" that other people made up. The textbooks written on color are wonderful tools to help understand the way color works. **But remember, there is no such thing as right or wrong in color choices for your artwork. Absolutely, those choices are a matter of personal expression, meaning—if it looks good to you, it's the right choice.**

I cringe when I hear a person say that they are going to use colors they hate just to get out of their comfort zone. Why? The project won't get finished. Why do it? Instead, explore more colors, hues, shades, and combinations of the colors you love. You will be happier this way. Trust me.

We begin a project with the design, the black lines that form our piece. At this step, we most likely have color choices earmarked in our heads, but that's a step we haven't yet taken. For now, concentrate on designing without the confusion of color choices. Make several copies of the picture.

Now, it's time to color. Do several different color drawings for more options. You may discover new color ideas if you allow yourself the time to experiment. Colors integrated into a pattern look different then when they stand alone in a black or white field. Always keep in mind that you will be stitching these colors. Fill in the drawing with marks that look like stitches. This will help you work through a project before you even get to your machine.

When you are satisfied with your color choices, make stitch samples. Color pencil drawings and stitched colored threads are two very different animals. At this point, you can experiment with different stitches, colors, and types/textures of thread. Once you are happy with the stitch samples, you can procede with the confidence that you will be pleased with your art.

Thread Painting MADE EASY ~ TERRY WHITE

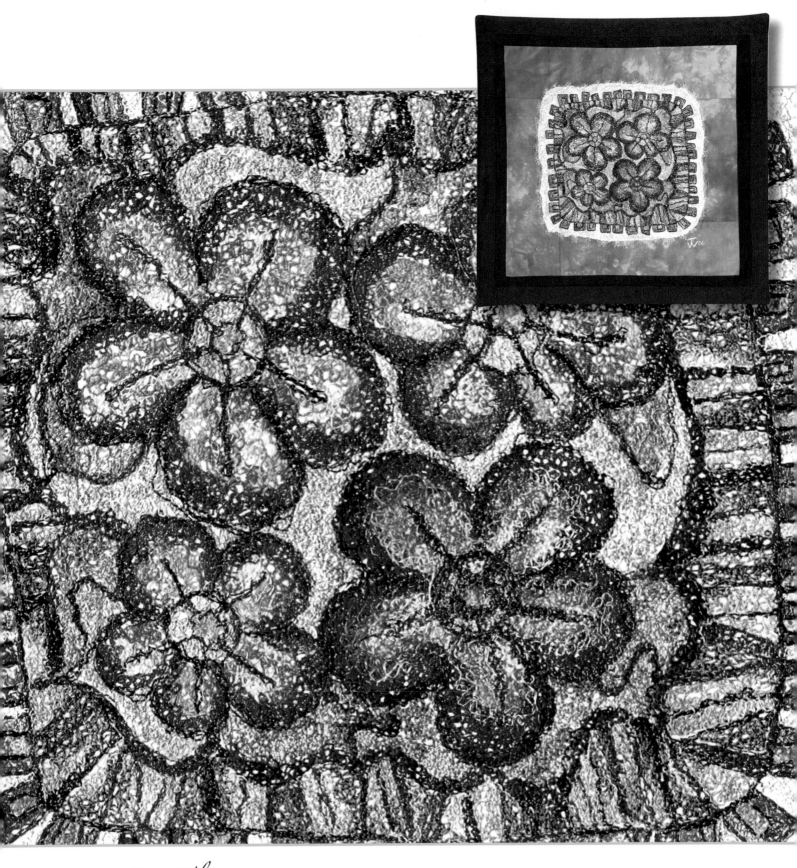

Posy Tile was so much fun, I used only vibrant YLI cotton machine quilting threads and a circular stitch. When traveling from one area to another, stitch in a serpentine stitch. This cuts down on the jump stitches. If you look closely, you can see that two threads were used simultaneously to achieve these colors.

Thread Painting MADE EASY ~ **TERRY WHITE**

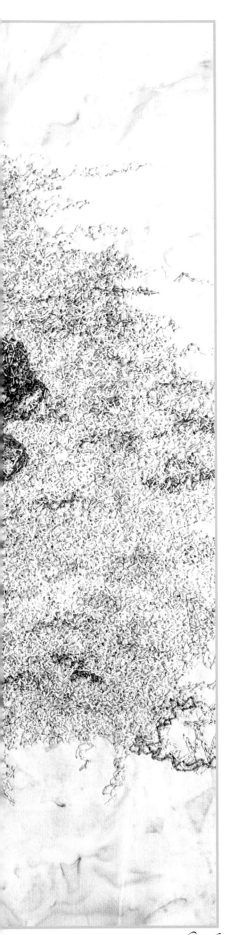

LESSON 5~ *The Mushroom*

The Mushroom is stitched with **circular** and **serpentine stitches.** The beauty is in the thread. Variegated color threads are created by artists and designers with a wonderful understanding of color. The mixes in these threads are absolutely beautiful and often surprising. Just using these threads is like a class in the use of color.

I began this piece with a fabric in mind, a commercially dyed, marble effect cotton. I used the colors from the fabric to stitch the sky. I made the stitch less and less dense as it approached the edges of the work.

This design begins with a simple line drawing. With this piece, the shapes rather than the lines are most important. Color the design with pencils to indicate the colors and contrasts of the shapes.

Some of the variegated threads used share common colors. When stitched side by side, those threads interweave and blend, which obliterates distinct lines.

A single stitch form is used in this project, which lends the piece an impressionistic look. Texture is the emphasis here.

Start with the cap of the mushroom. Use a **circular stitch** in a variegated lilac/ blue/pink thread with a long color change. As the color changes, separate the colors by moving to the next area.

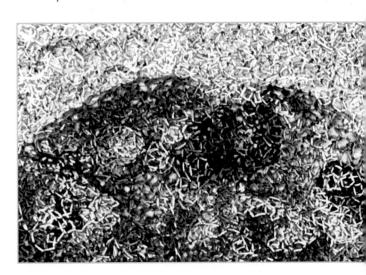

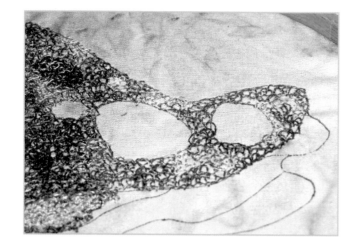

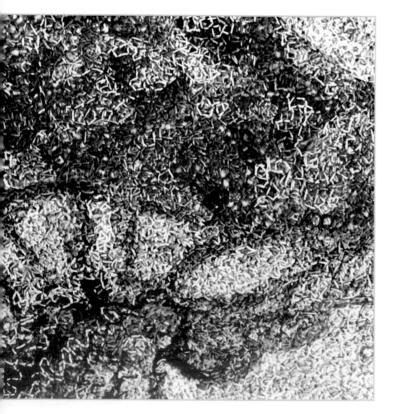

Filling in the cap's spots with different threads created more contrast than I wanted. After the spots were stitched, I **overstitched** in an open circular fashion with the first thread I used. This subdued the contrast of the colors and softly blended one shape to the next.

Stitch openly when laying down the different areas of color. This creates the opportunity to add more colors and more blending.

On the underside of the mushroom cap, stitch along the lines in darker colors. In the bigger areas, stitch in lighter threads. Include interesting colors to highlight your design. The colors themselves aren't even necessarily important compared to the contrasts which outline the shapes.

When stitching a design that is larger than the hoop, complete the area in the hoop and then re-hoop the next area to stitch.

The drawing was colored in with general impressions of where the color contrasts would be. It was colored in a circular manner. When it comes to thread painting the image, you have total freedom to choose the threads as you go along. This is PLAYTIME. By the way, I'm informed that if you find a mushroom like this, don't eat it.

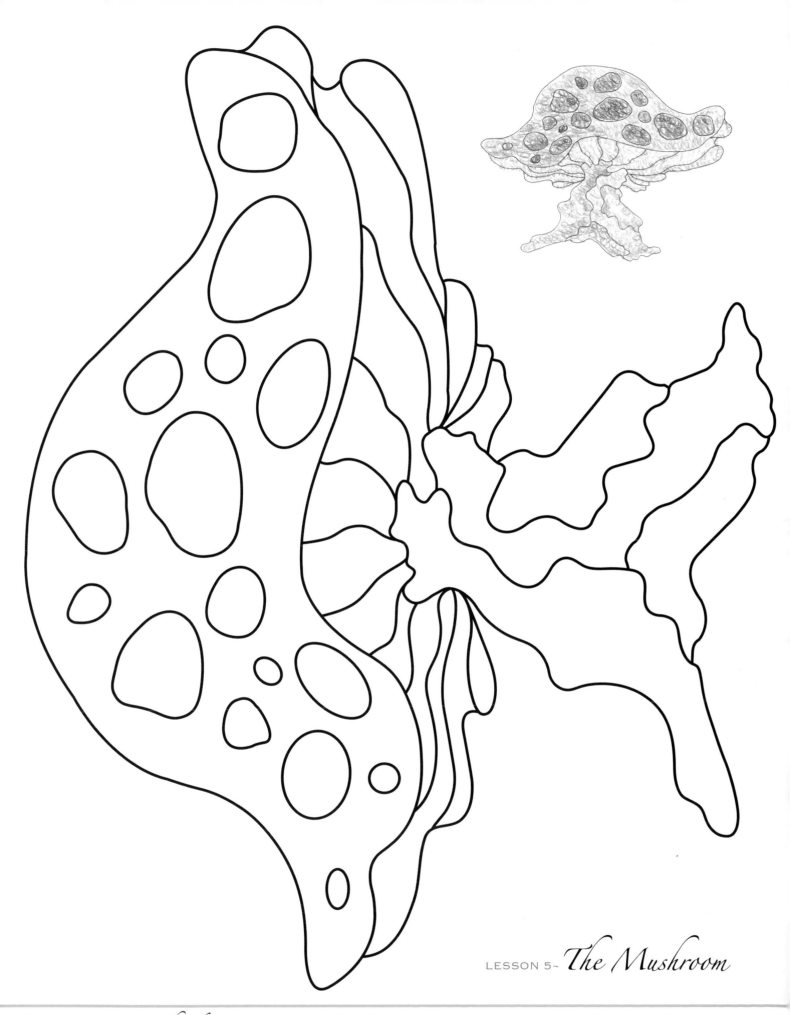

LESSON 5~ *The Mushroom*

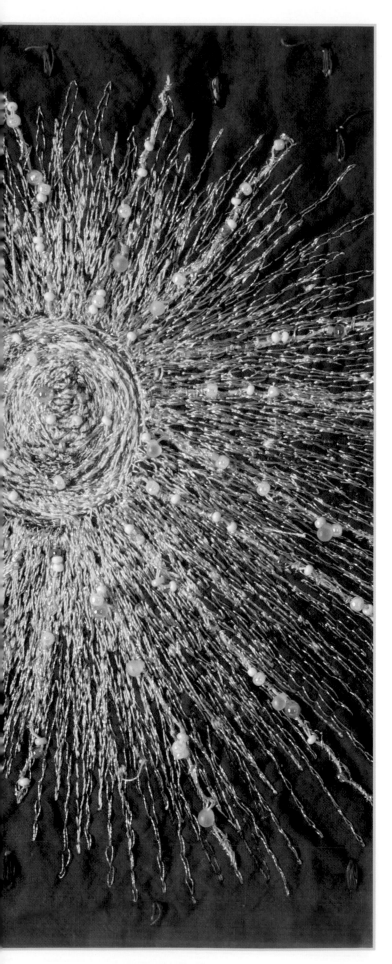

METALLIC THREADS

Metallics are the divas of the thread world. They are gorgeous despite being sometimes a little difficult to work with. If you treat them right, however, they will perform beautifully.

The thread companies really know their products. Their instructional guidelines are the result of extensive testing. For the best results, we need only to follow their directions. The tips here are all things I have learned either directly from the thread companies or from my own experimentation. I have seen many students struggle with these threads, only to later learn just how great these threads are when handled correctly. They're truly worth the effort.

If your metallic thread frequently breaks, pay attention to where the break is occurring. If the breakage occurs in the tension discs, you lower your tension. If your thread is breaking at the needle, either the needle or the fabric could be causing the problem.

To help you through the transition, I've made a list of suggestions for dealing with metallic threads.

Use a needle appropriate for the thread and fabric. I use a 90/14 embroidery needle for almost everything I thread paint. However, some situations call for a metallica needle, like stitching on a dense or rough fabric. The eye of this needle is bigger than an embroidery needle and the front groove is deeper, which better protects the metal thread from the surrounding fabric.

Choose an appropriate fabric and stabilizer. Heavy, dense, or rough fabrics make it very difficult to thread paint with metallics. **Think friction.** The action of the thread passing back and forth through a rough or dense fabric can fray and break the thread. It is also difficult to use metallic threads on fused fabrics unless the fusible used is very light. Even then, you probably want to use a metallic big needle and a wrapped metallic thread.

Lower the tension settings on the machine. Anytime you use these threads in your machine, you want to set your tension very low. Open up the tension discs so that the thread flows freely and doesn't floss between the tension discs causing friction and breakage.

Use an appropriate thread delivery system. For the most part, try to stitch off the side of the spool. This helps to prevent twisting, tension problems, and breakage of the thread.

Use the correct bobbin thread. When working with metallics, the best bobbin threads are soft and have texture which will grip the thread without breaking it. I personally use YLI Soft Touch, Sulky polyester bobbin thread, and OESD bobbin thread.

Choose stitches that work with the thread. Metallic thread is beautiful. Let it shine! Use longer stitches that allow for more surface area and more shine. Flat metallics need even longer stitches to obtain that maximum glittery effect. Also, longer stitches will give you fewer problems with the bobbin area.

Keep it cool. The heat from your sewing machine light can cause flat metallic threads to stretch and break. If you are stitching for a long period of time, check for heat coming off of the light. Take little breaks so your thread doesn't. High humidity can exacerbate any friction problem between the metallic thread and the metal parts of your sewing machine. If you can, turn on the air conditioner in hot weather.

Machine operator should be set to a slow and steady speed. The machine operator is YOU. Stitch slowly. What I mean by this is—stitch slowly. Stitch more slowly than you usually do. Okay? Stitch at a steady speed and make gentle movements. Rough movements can break your thread.

Machine operator's brain set on low tension. Relax your mind and relax your body. This will help with the smooth movements for smooth stitching.

Machine operator's mind set on PLAY. Do I need to clarify? It's PLAYTIME!

Thread Painting MADE EASY ~ **TERRY WHITE**

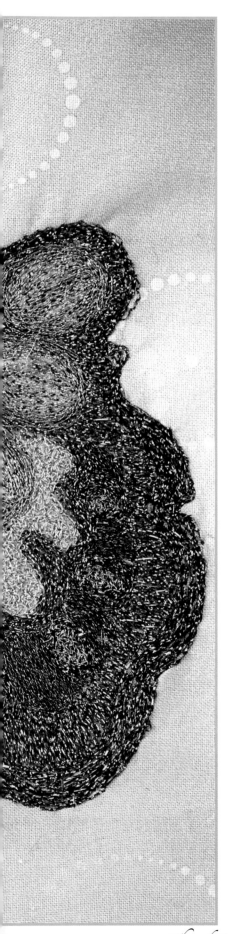

LESSON 6~ *Luminous Moth*

Luminous Moth was stitched completely with metallics, including hologram flat metallic and wrapped metallic threads. This is one shiny moth dressed up for a ball!

Materials

THREADS USED

1. Dark teal wrapped metallic – Superior Metallic #30
2. Grass green wrapped metallic – YLI Fine Metallic # G12
3. Light green wrapped metallic – Superior Metallic #24
4. Gold wrapped metallic – Superior Metallic #7
5. Copper hologram flat metallic – Sulky Holoshimmer #6011
6. Purple wrapped metallic – Sulky Metallic #7050
7. Pink wrapped metallic – Sulky Metallic #7012
8. Dark pink hologram flat metallic – Sulky Holoshimmer #6054
9. Medium blue hologram flat metallic – YLI Kaleidoscope #003

Fabric

Soft 100 percent cotton with pale pink print 14" square. Use any color you would like. The color will show through in some areas of the work.

Let's Stitch!

Test each thread on the exact fabric you will be stitching on. This way any problems you might encounter can be worked out ahead of time.

Match the thread number with the area on the design of the same number. This is thread painting by number!

1. Stitch the head with three rows of **contour stitches**. When you try to fill in an area with this thread, it works best to stitch the whole area and then go back over it a second and third time. The bottom of the moth is stitched in smooth contour stitches.

2. Stitch the moth's cap and the eye rings in **satin stitch**. Stitch the body section next to the moth's bottom in a **smooth contour stitch**.

3. Stitch the moth's middle and the egg shapes in **smooth contour stitches**.

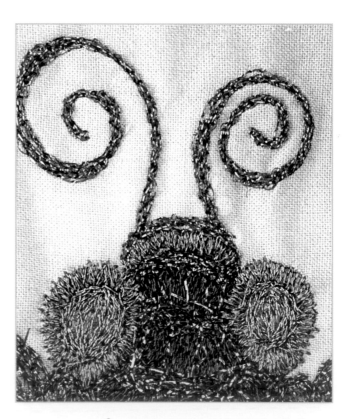

4. Stitch the area marked #4 in **random circular stitches**.

5. Stitch the antennae and outline the cap in **long and short contour stitches**. Stitch the collar in **smooth contour stitches**. Go slowly using big stitches.

6. Stitch the areas marked #6 in **long and short contour stitches**.

7. **Satin stitch** the eyes. Outline the green egg shapes with **long and short contour stitches**. Stitch the small egg shapes in **random circular stitching**.

8. Fill in the area marked #8 with **long and short contour stitches**.

9. **Long and short contour stitch** in all areas marked #9. Outline little pink egg shapes as well. Add a zig-zag line detail in the purple area near the top of the wings.

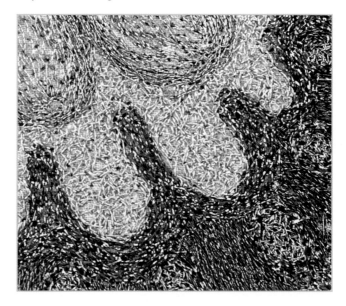

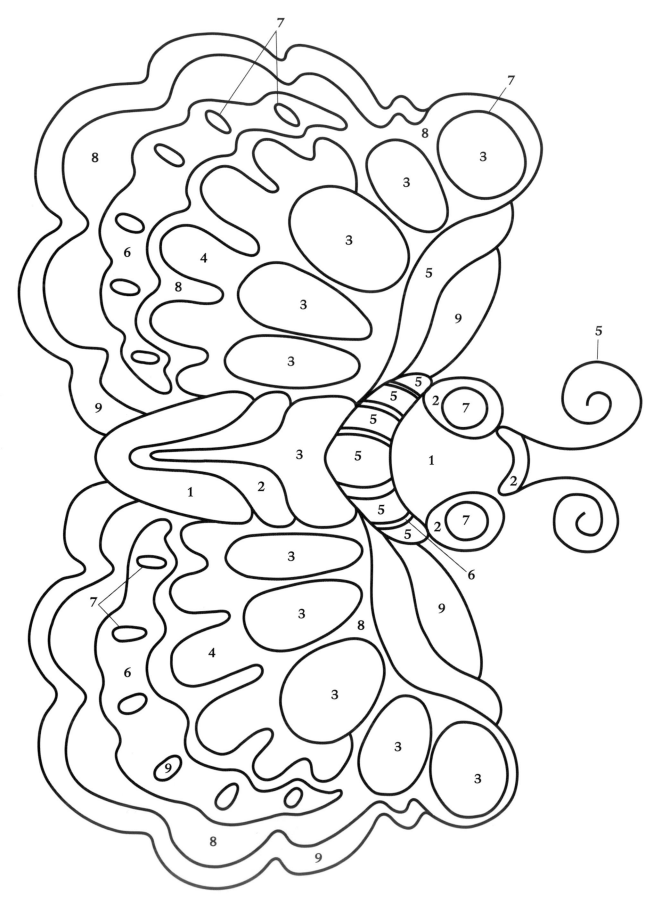

ABOVE: This version of *Luminous Moth* was stitched with an even mix of cotton and metallic stitched areas. I like the contrast of the glitzy against the natural look of the cotton. YLI variegated cotton threads were used.

RIGHT: This version of *Luminous Moth* (detail) is almost entirely stitched in Valdani threads with just an accent of gold metallic.

Glass Watergarden This quilt was stitched on a hand-dyed fabric by Quilter's Treasure. The design was stitched directly onto the fabric. It is a mix of cotton and metallic threads. My beading by machine technique was used to add glass beads. The work was inspired by some of the beautiful glass vessels seen at art galleries. Looking closely you can see how the flat copper metallic thread looks next to the turquoise rayon threads.

LESSON 7~ *Stitched Backgrounds*

When a design is densely stitched, some distortion will occur around the design. If the work is going to be quilted, this is usually not a problem. The quilting process will fix it. However, if the work will not be quilted, some interesting background stitching can be used to ease out the puckers.

The background stitches should start out reasonably dense around the design, then open out gradually towards the edges of the work. Besides solving your distortion problems, this technique will help make your project even more intricate and interesting.

The background stitch can be anything you can imagine: a grid, small motifs, repetitive designs, various size polka dots, etc. Using variegated threads can add a lot of interest here. You can change the color of the background fabric, create an environment for the motif, or even frame it. Background stitching is yet another outlet for your creative energy.

ABOVE, RIGHT: *A Tasty Cup of Tea was stitched on muslin. This way the threads alone color the design. The background was colored in with colored pencils. The threads used are YLI cotton variegated machine quilting threads. I used two threads through the eye of the needle.*

RIGHT: *The background design for Fancy Pear was stitched with bronze and copper threads using a stem stitch. Bronze beads were attached at the intersections.*

Moth Tile was stitched using a mix of threads from Superior. Cotton variegates were used in the main design. Detailing and some overstitching was done with metallics. The frame was stitched in rows of decorative sewing machine stitches with the cotton variegated threads. Rows of decorative machine stitches would make an interesting background.

The background in MOTH TILE was stitched in gold metallic and cotton variegated threads in a crosshatch pattern.

The Finch Was Framed was stitched on two different fabrics. The bird was stitched on Osnaburg, then pressed, squared up, cut, and stitched in the center of the frame. The frame was stitched on a heavier homespun fabric. If the entire design was stitched on one fabric, there would have been distortion and the frame would not be as square. This project is stitched with Superior's King Tut cotton variegated threads.

Thread Painting MADE EASY ~ **TERRY WHITE**

LESSON 8~ *All the Stitches*

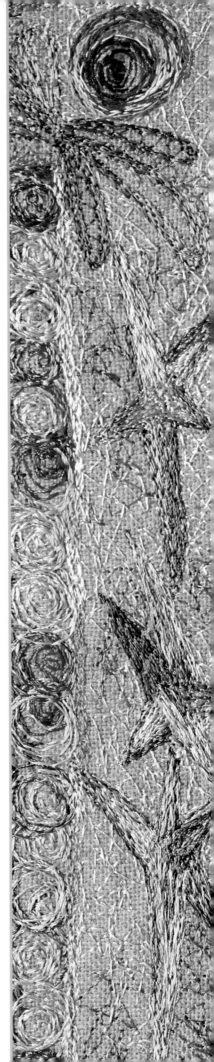

For this final project, I have incorporated many of the stitches from the glossary into one piece. The threads (all from WonderFil) are varied in order to add a textural contrast. This decorative panel is called THE SUN IN THE MORNING AND THE MOON AT NIGHT.

Trace the design from the drawings. The numbers correspond to the thread colors listed in the color key. See the small colored versions shown on the design page.

Materials

I used natural color drapery linen for this work that I colorwashed with Tsukineko® dye paints. This gave me the color I wanted showing through the open stitches.

The fabric was washed and left damp. The dyes were thinned with water and applied with a big paint brush. When the fabric was completely colored, a hot dry iron was applied with a pressing cloth to set the color in the fabric. Then it was washed and pressed again.

Anytime I work with a natural fiber, I wash it, sometimes twice if there is a lot of shrinkage.

Trace the design onto your fabric with a permanent archival quality pen. I used a big point to draw onto the fabric to better see the markings, though I did have to overstitch some areas to cover the marks.

For the stabilizer, use a non-woven interfacing like Shirtmaker.

The bobbin thread used was Deco-bob.

THREADS USED

1. Dark purple variegated rayon – Mirage SD10
2. Pale variegated rayon – Mirage SD18
3. Red variegated cotton – Silco SCM30
4. Orange/gold/brown variegated rayon – Mirage SD31
5. Yellow/orange variegated cotton – Silco SCM11
6. Warm yellow variegated rayon – MirageSD36
7. Rose wrapped metallic – Metallic 8835
8. Gold metallic – Metallic 8858
9. Turquoise variegated cotton – Silco SCM16 for the crosshatch background
10. Dark blue variegated rayon – MirageSD37
11. Light blue variegated rayon – MirageSD13
12. Silver metallic – Metallic881
13. Medium blue variegated cotton – SilcoSCM18
14. Dark blue to silver variegated rayon – MirageSD5
15. Solid aqua blue rayon – Accent 944
16. Red cotton – SilcoSC29
17. Green variegated rayon – Mirage SD1
18. Green to dark green variegated rayon – Mirage SD16
19. Dark blue green variegated rayon – Accent ACM3
20. Blue to yellow variegated rayon – Mirage SD25
21. Bright multicolor variegated rayon – Accent ACM38
22. Dark blue to turquoise variegated rayon – Accent ACM4

Let's Stitch!

The Sun

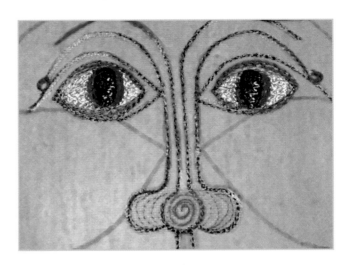

When doing a face, always start with the main features first—the eyes. Their expression sets the tone for the rest of the work. The outline of the eyes was done in a **running stitch**. The rest was done in a **smooth contour stitch**. When outlining large areas like this one, stitch about an inch at a time going back and forth. Then move to the next inch and repeat. It is much easier to control the stitching in a small section of the line.

The forehead and areas of the lower face have **crosshatch stitching**. These decorative stitches add an appropriate embellishment to this fantasy face.

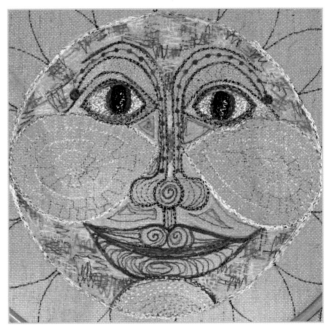

The cheek is done with rows of **ladder stitching**. First, stitch the outlines of the cheeks and the concentric rows. Then, go back and stitch the little lines across.

The nose and eyebrows have rows of connected **French knots**.

Many areas are simply done in an **outline stitch**. Look at the photos for guidance on these areas.

The sun's rays use two repeated motifs. The gold ray is first stitched with the red thread. Then the warm yellow is stitched in the squares with a **crosshatch stitch**. Then, gold thread is stitched with an **x** in the center of each square.

The red ray is first **outline stitched** with the yellow/orange variegate. Then, three connected **French knots** are stitched in the sides with the red thread. The red circle is stitched next. The yellow/orange variegate is used to stitch around the red circle. Then, the red metallic thread is stitched in the remaining triangle shape.

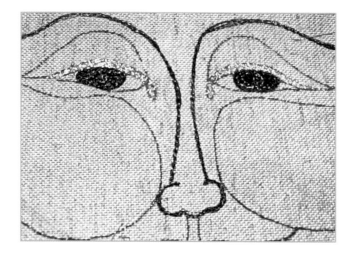

The Moon

Begin the moon with the eyes. Use the dark blue for the eyeball and the silver for the inner lid using **smooth contour stitches**.

The details of the eyebrows, nose, and mouth are **outline stitched**. Follow the drawing for guidance.

Large areas of the face are stitched in **spiral stitch** and **serpentine stitch**.

The eyelids are striped with the medium blue and purple threads. The cheeks are stitched in **ladder stitch**, the same as with the sun face.

The area around the moon is stitched in **serpentine stitches**.

The ring around the moon is stitched exactly the same as the eyelids of the face.

Background

The background area is stitched in **crosshatch** with **#9** turquoise thread.

The stars are stitched in **satin stitch** with two threads through the eye of the needle. Those threads are marked **#11** and **#12** on the list. The stars are outlined with aqua thread in several rows of **outline stitch**, then outlined again with the dark blue thread.

The blossoms are stitched in **smooth contour stitches**. The center is stitched first with the metallic red and then **overstitched** with red cotton thread. The outer ring is stitched in warm yellow variegated thread, then it is outlined with the red cotton thread.

The leaves are stitched with the green variegate then outlined with the warm yellow, then again outlined with dark green.

The border of the panel starts with the **spiral stitch** in rows using the bright color mix variegated thread.

The next row is **chain stitched** with the warm yellow variegate.

The stars are stitched with the dark to light blue variegate in **smooth contour stitches**.

The next row is **chain stitched** in the warm yellow exactly as the second row.

Fill in the background of the stars with **triangle stitching** with the blue to yellow variegated thread.

Next, stitch the leaf sets with the dark variegated green. Stitch the circle blossoms with the red variegate.

The corner flowers are stitched exactly like those in the center of the panel.

The edge is finished with three rows of decorative machine stitching. For the first and third rows, stitch down four thick decorative threads with an **open stitch**, using the multi-cord foot on your machine. The middle row is stitched with the bright color variegated in a **diamond-shaped stitch**.

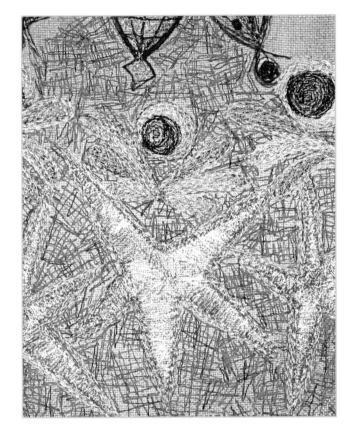

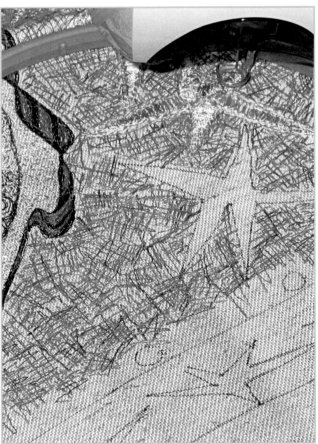

LESSON 8 ~ *All the Stitches*

LESSON 9~ *Animals*

This chapter is more of a show-and-tell than a project. Most people love their pet (or their neighbor's, or their brother's, or that one on TV, etc.) and don't want a picture of someone else's animal. That's why it is so important to personalize this lesson. For every kind of animal, the fur, feathers, wool, or scales suggest different thread and stitch combinations. To begin, study the animal. Then experiment with stitches and thread combinations until you have the right mix.

This is a freehand drawing of Karl based on these three photographs.

I think it is important to mention copyright here. Photos of animals in books are copyrighted. You will have to get permission to use the photo for your work. I like to take pictures of animals in my yard or the zoo. In my case, I can draw so I never directly trace from a photograph.

This dog is Karl. He belongs to my neighbors Charles and Sanna. The photo was theirs, but they gave me permission to thread paint him for my book. Luckily, YLI Thread Company sent me the Monet threads you see, which happen to perfectly match Karl. If you aren't confident in your drawing skills and you want to stitch an animal, here is a great way to get your image. This is a graphic designer's trick. Enlarge your photo to the size you need. Make a grayscale copy and a black-and-white copy. This way you can trace the main areas without the distraction of color. When you thread paint, use your original photo to guide you in the colors.

After drawing Karl, I traced the main lines onto my muslin using a light box and a .01 Micron Pigma pen. Now, the work is ready to hoop with stabilizer and stitch.

As I've said, I used YLI's Monét threads for this project. They are fuzzy and gave a wonderful texture to the project. Also, I used YLI polyester variegates and a cotton variegate.

I always start with the animal's eyes and work my way through the main facial features. If the expression isn't right, I trash it and start over. Like I've said before, it is crucial to test your thread combinations and stitch varieties before starting the project. Different types of threads require different tension adjustments. For instance, the Monét thread stitched with the loosest tension and the polyester thread needed a tighter tension. I always adjust the machine as I change threads.

I used a 100/16 needle to accommodate the Monét. I didn't change needles for the polyester thread because of the amount of overstitching this project required. To get a raised texture, I needed the 100/16 needle's strength to prevent thread breakage. Believe me, holes won't show through all that dense stitching. Also, the natural fibers of the fabric will absorb the holes without showing.

It is very important to be mindful of stitch sequence. For instance, I wanted to begin with the eyes to make sure I captured the right expression, but first I stitched the fur around the eyes. Doing it this way allowed the eyes to snuggle into the fur, making the finished piece look more lifelike.

As you can see, the direction of the stitches is important even when stitching with a white thread.

Once you're satisfied with the expression in the eyes, the rest of the portrait will come together easily.

LEFT: *Here is Karl all stitched out—only the background is boring. Time to stitch the background. I used blues and greens to create a strong contrast with Karl.*

OPPOSITE: *For the background, a crosshatch stitch was used: first in a blue variegate, then an orange variegate, and finally a turquoise variegate. All three areas was then overstitched in crosshatch with a green variegate.*

A Renaissance of Peace is a mixed-techniques quilt. This work was done over a period of two years while I was working 55-hour weeks, owned three teenagers, and was preparing to marry for the last time. This was my daydream. I just wanted a little peace!

Fish These are details from an unfinished fish quilt. Aren't fish beautiful with their many colors and textures? They are easier than mammals because their eyes are expressionless.

I colored the fish with circular stitching and then overstitched with a clamshell stitch.

I achieved a lot of texture in the plants by using every type of thread and stitch I could think of.

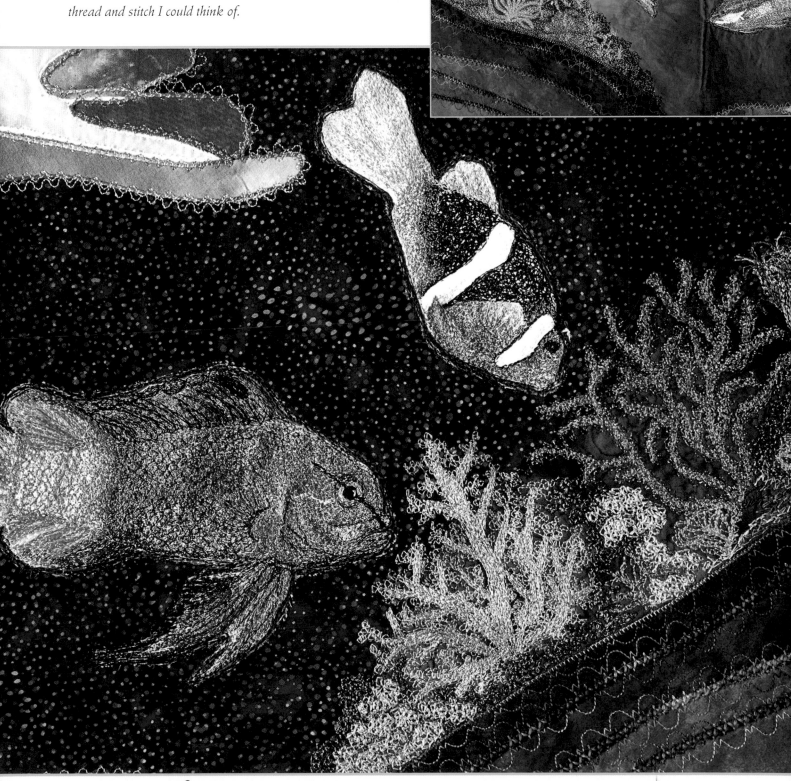

LESSON 10~ *Wearable Art*

When I sew clothes, I like to make them special. My grandmother used to make Mardi-Gras costumes. When the party was over, we got to play Dress-Up with them. As my children were growing up, costumes and doll clothes provided a great excuse for me to have a ton of fun sewing. Now, teaching in the creative textile field gives me plenty of opportunities to still play Dress-Up. In fact, that's precisely what we do whenever we go to quilting and sewing events. Let's explore some ideas that use thread painting on clothes.

African Jacket This garment utilizes a combination of techniques. The main fabric is heavy woven raw silk. The cat mask was thread painted onto muslin and then appliquéd to the jacket. The other animals were stitched from a computer-generated embroidery card onto Osnaburg. A little border was created around each one with a wing needle and an heirloom stitch on the sewing machine. The edges were then frayed. The separate designs were moved around on the jacket until the placement looked just right. To create the vines, decorative sewing machine stitches, beautiful yarns, and applied Ultrasuede® leaves were used. Those finishing touches really bring the various elements together. There is a lot going on in this jacket, but by controlling the color palette it doesn't appear busy.

Joker Jacket (page 101, detail), Okay, this one is a little over the top. In my defense, I was going to Las Vegas for the first time for a sewing convention. I thought this was what one should wear. The fabric has an open weave. It drapes nicely and is very soft. Because the fabric could not support this much

Thread Painting MADE EASY ~ **TERRY WHITE**

stitching, the clown was stitched onto muslin and appliquéd to the back of the jacket. After stitching the image, the fabric was about an eighth of an inch around the design and appliquéd with a satin stitch in silver metallic thread. For the appliqué, a very stiff tearaway stabilizer was used on the inside of the jacket. It is important to consider the drape of the garment before placing your designs. Make sure that stiff appliqués don't interfere with the hang of your garment.

Viva Las Vegas This handbag is the essential accessory to accentuate the JOKER JACKET. After all, what else would match?

Here are some of my blue jean jacket designs and details. *Gyrobum* belongs to my husband, Scot. To celebrate his successful building of an ultralight aircraft, I decorated his flight jacket.

JazzCat is all mine.

Thar Be Dragons Here (opposite) is a kimono the body of which is a fabric mix of lamé, nylon, and acetate. It was a beautiful novelty fabric, which can't be ironed and frayed badly. The separate design elements were stitched on mulsin, and then applied to the fabric.

Open Blossom (detail), was stitched to the back of a jacket with a couched copper knitted cord and decorative sewing machine stitches. A beautiful yarn was wrapped around the design and couched down. The copper cord and yarn were both extended into the back of the piece and couched. A button accents the edge of the circle. The jacket was made of a crinkled iridescent metallic fabric.

I always face the appliqué before stitching it to the jacket. That way the design can be removed for laundering or if the owner wants to use it on some other garment.

Faced Appliqué – A piece of muslin fabric is placed over the design with right sides together. The fabrics are stitched together and then trimmed to ⅛" all around the seam. The muslin is slashed with a 3" slice in the center of the circle. The work is turned right-side-out and pressed.

SECTION III
Compendium

TROUBLESHOOTING

Most of these issues have been addressed in other sections of this book, but they're collected here in one place as a reminder. I'll note the problem and give several possibilities as to the cause.

You find the needle pushing the fabric into the needle plate:
- ~ The fabric might not be taut in the hoop and may need to be re-hooped.
- ~ The needle might be dull and may need to be changed.
- ~ There might be too much overstitching.

Too much bobbin thread is coming up to the top of the work:
- ~ The bobbin thread might be too lightweight. If so, change to a heavier thread.
- ~ You might be stitching too fast and moving the work too slowly. Slow down the machine.
- ~ You might be jerking the work back and forth under the needle. Rough motions pull up the thread. Relax your movements.
- ~ You might be moving the hoop too quickly while creating curves. So slow down your movements.
- ~ The top thread tension might be too tight. If so, lower the tension setting.
- ~ Make sure that your bobbin thread hasn't "jumped" the tension discs.
- ~ There might be too much overstitching.
- ~ You might be trying to stitch through too many layers of fabric or fusibles. If so, try a bigger needle.

Thread Painting MADE EASY ~ **TERRY WHITE**

~ The top thread may be stuck. It could either be twisted up at the thread cap or caught on its own spool.

~ The bobbin may be almost out of thread which causes it to come up with the top thread. If so, change to a full bobbin.

Too much top thread is looping on the bottom of the work:

~ The thread tension is too loose. Tighten it.

~ The top thread may have jumped out of tension. Re-thread it.

Your machine is making a "clunking" noise at the point of stitching:

~ Change to a new needle.

~ Clean out the bobbin case area.

~ There might be too much overstitching. Stop overstitching.

Your threads are breaking:

~ The thread tension could be too tight. If so, lower the thread tension.

~ The thread delivery system may cause too much drag on the thread.

~ The thread may be twisting and breaking. If so, change the delivery system.

~ The thread may be caught up somewhere, for instance on the edge of the spool pin or a burr on the side of the spool.

~ The needle may be too small.

~ The fabric may be too rough.

Moth at Rest was stitched on a very busy print from Quilters Treasure. I had to draw the outline of my design on the back of the fabric. Then I outline stitched the moth with black thread in the bobbin. That allowed me to see the thread lines on the fabric top. We have moths like these in our yard.

DISCOVERING YOUR ARTIST WITHIN

You can design your own thread paintings. You wouldn't have picked up this book if you didn't have design ability. I'm speaking to the both of you—the artist who has no doubt she can draw and the artist who doesn't know she can draw—when I say here are some simple exercises to get you started.

Exercise 1: Doodled Letter

We draw whenever we doodle, scribble, or write words. Each person has unique marks that she makes. For instance, every individual when writing her name interprets the shape of the lines in a letter of the alphabet differently. That is why signatures are so unique.

Use a pencil and a blank white sheet of paper. Draw the first letter of your name in the middle of the sheet. Make it about four inches tall. Now, take another sheet of white paper and draw it again, only this time, relax and give it a little flair. **Remember, I didn't say write the first letter of your name. I said to draw it.** We love the first letter of our name; we draw it all the time.

Now, switch to a fine-point black pen. Without thinking too much, quickly trace your drawing. It's not important to stay on the original line. Now start to doodle or scribble around the letter. Maybe you like solid forms that lend weight to the design. Maybe you choose to embellish it with vines and leaves. You may love to draw squares, triangles, checkerboards, or dots. Stop looking at the image as a letter and begin to look at it as the basis of your design. Again, don't think too much and enjoy the process of making the marks. It is almost a childish thing to do. We both know when you were younger you drew all the time without judging yourself.

Without realizing it, you are taking a basic design, the letter, and adding your own elements to it.

Now, let's say you like some of what you did, but some of your lines or additions bother you. Trace what you like onto another piece of paper. Continue on.

My Springtime, 54" x 40". FROM THE COLLECTION OF MARY FOWLER.

The purpose of this exercise was to show you how much fun it can be to draw. The more you draw, the more you can distinguish how you see things and interpret them.

Exercise 2: Look Around

Scot has a theory that people know what they like when they see it. It's a matter of experience (experimental play) to know how to achieve it in one's own work. You must identify what appeals to you.

Get your old stacks of magazines. It doesn't really matter what kind. Start ripping out images that you like. Does the ad have a cool border graphic or an image with incredible color? As you rip, write a little note to yourself on that page describing what you like about it.

If you don't have stacks of magazines, go through your books or go to the library. In the library you may go to the garden section, architecture, animal, or art books. Don't forget about the children's books. Rather than ripping out the pages, slide in a little note of paper with your comments marking the pages that appeal to you.

After you have had about an hour's worth of fun doing this, start looking at what you've gathered. Now, organize all the color images you liked (all the graphics that appealed to you, etc.) Is there a commonality in the color scheme? You may find that there are several different color groupings that appeal to you again and again. Don't be surprised if your wardrobe or your fabric stash reflects this. This may help you see color combinations that you haven't tried yet. Maybe you notice you like impressionistic landscapes or hard-line drawings. This will help you get to know what you like and also help you express it in your work.

Exercise 3: Discover Yourself

Start with five pieces of blank white paper and a black fine-point marker. In less than a minute, draw a fast doodle on each sheet of paper. Then, look at all the doodles side by side. You will see that you repeat shapes. The movements of the lines are similar. These shapes are determined by the size of your hand, whether you are right- or left-handed, whether you like to work big or small, and your personality. Pull out the doodle that you like best and begin to develop it as a drawing. You can draw small elements that you like from your reference materials (gathered from the previous exercise), or embellish with repetitions of the lines and shapes you drew yourself. Your lines may suggest buildings, trees, or people. You're learning and playing with your personal preferences, which is the only way to develop your own work.

Now that you have some interesting black-and-white drawings, add color. Use some of the color combinations that you liked in the previous exercise.

Whatever you liked in your work, do it again and again. Develop the shapes and lines and develop your color combinations.

When you make a drawing to thread paint, you want to start with a simple line drawing. The threads and stitches paint the design, filling it out. So, even if you are an accomplished artist, you will start with a line drawing. If you create an elaborate design that you carefully and beautifully color in with colored pencils, you will be limiting yourself once you begin to stitch. You will try to mimic every pencil stroke and you'll not be involved with the immediate process of thread painting. This process is like painting on canvas. You want to leave yourself open to the unexpected stitches that pop into your head. Allow the colors to do things you don't expect.

Unexpected Stitches and Surprises

The more you do, the more you learn and the more you will know. Some of the stitches or color combinations that I deliberately use now, originated from mistakes or surprises. I take full credit for them because I took the time to experiment and I paid attention to the results.

Developing your style is just that—a process of development.

Play is very important. Sometimes, I have an idea, but not enough time to develop it into a project at the moment. I'll play with the idea in the fabrics and threads I envision. I'm happy later when that play turns out to be the center of a great project. Or, I'm happy because I didn't waste too much time on that dog!

"TAKE CARE OF YOURSELF"

Before starting your work, be sure that your stitching environment is good for you. A really good lighting system is necessary. I have an Ott-Lite® lamp. My Christmas present several years ago was a really good office chair with lumbar support.

"TIME TO GET UP"

I keep a clock on my sewing table facing me. I try to get up at least every 30 minutes or so. It's good for me. I walk around, stretch, get a drink of water, fold a load of laundry, defrost the fish for dinner, paint a wall, or weed the garden. I get my little tasks done around the house in my "it's time to get up" time. Thread painting is not the same as piecing a quilt. There is no getting up to iron or cut new pieces. You may find yourself holding a single position for hours as you forget the rest of the world. This leads to nothing but sore joints.

"BLINK AND BREATHE"

In class, people are always saying, "Don't forget to breathe." Well, blinking is important, too. When I really get into the zone, I'll find my eyes are watering because I've forgotten to blink.

Nurture the Nest

Nurture the nest and the nest will nurture you.

ROBBY CHRISTIAN, DECEMBER 2005

My daughter said those encouraging words to me, while I was painting the kitchen in response to some big health issues and emotional drama. They made so much sense to me.

As I was cleaning up in the sewing studio one day, I was gathering up stray threads. I started to twist the threads until they looked like a birds nest. I dropped what I was doing and started making little eggs with different techniques. Finally, I simply wrapped a cotton ball with variegated blue crochet cotton.

I've made several of these since. These little nests find their way to women who appreciate the message.

A Midsummer's Daydream is a cartoon of Robby and her little son AJ (AJ is represented by the little bird). I drew it from a photograph of Robby taken when she was two years old. In case you're wondering, we called her Birdie for many years. The work looks like a page from a book of fairy tales. I painted the damp background fabric with Tsukineko dye paints. To achieve the aura around the fairy, I kept adding little drops of water so that the paint would leach out into the background. When the colors were just right, I arrested the process by heat. Using an iron, I set the paint. I then drew the design and thread painted it. The work is quilted with gold metallic thread from Superior.

Resources

TERRY'S WEB SITE

www.threadpaint.com

This is where you can see class offerings and galleries of work.

TWTHREADWORKS

www.twthreadworks.com

Source for WonderFil Threads, Morgan No-Slip hoop, classes on CD, patterns, etc.

WONDERFIL® THREADS

www.wonderfil.net

The trouble shooting information is very good, with helpful tips on each thread. There is a teacher resource list.

YLI CORPORATION

www.ylicorp.com

The "Thread of Truth" is a very thorough technical document with everything one would want to know about the structure and content of threads. It can be downloaded and printed.

SUPERIOR THREADS

www.superiorthreads.com

The thread reference guide is very helpful and "Thread Facts" is a guide to using threads.

SULKY OF AMERICA

www.sulky.com

FAQ question and answers are very helpful.

ROBISON ANTON

www.robison-anton.com

Very good technical information on their products is provided.

FIBRE&STITCH ONLINE ZINE

www.fiberandstitch.com

This cool online magazine explores mixed techniques including paper, thread, and fiber.

QUILTSTREAM

www.quiltstream.com

This site is streaming video for free about all things quilty.

QUILTERS TREASURE

www.quilterstreasure.com

Hand-marbled fabrics are featured.

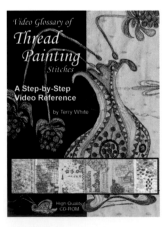

Companion CD-ROM video available from AQS
www.AmericanQuilter.com

About Terry White

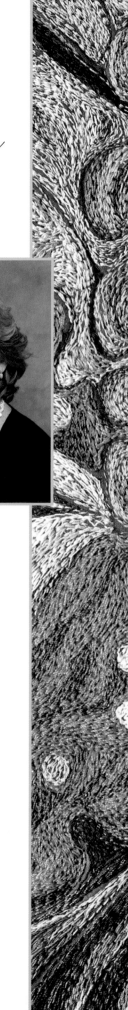

Terry has designed hand-embroidered items since she was in grade school. The study of historical and world embroidery has been one of her passions since she was allowed to go to the library by herself in the 7th grade.

To say that she is self-taught would be a mistake. Her contemporary embroidery designs have been inspired by Constance Howard's embroidery books, textile artists Gloria Vanderbilt (fiber collages), Ed Rossbach (structural textile work), Kaffe Fassett (needlepoint and color), and many others from the 1970s.

When Terry learned to quilt in 1978, she embellished her work with the hand needlework she knew. When her hands stopped working for her, she turned to the sewing machine. In 1996, she learned free-machine embroidery. Since then she has dedicated her time to developing techniques and designs that are as beautiful and texturally interesting as work done by hand.

Terry loves to teach her techniques to students across the country. She especially likes to help women see the potential for developing their own style with this very easy form of needlework.

Other AQS Books

This is only a small selection of the books available from the American Quilter's Society. AQS books are known worldwide for timely topics, clear writing, beautiful color photos, and accurate illustrations and patterns. The following books are available from your local bookseller, quilt shop, or public library.

#7602 us$26.95

#7071 us$22.95

#7610 us$26.95

#7607 us$26.95

#7609 us$19.95

#7492 us$22.95

#7012 us$19.95

#6519 us$21.95

#7486 us$22.95